THE
AWESOME
POWER
OF PRAYER

Best wishes from Sam
Sophie & Lawrence.

Ramat Rachael
15/9/09.

THE
AWESOME
POWER
OF PRAYER

SAM LARBIE

New Life Publishing Co.

Also by Sam Larbie and published by New Life Publishing Co:
Healing is Easy, 'cos of what Jesus has done

New Life Publishing Co.
Nottingham, England

First published by Alivia Media, 2002
This edition first published in the UK, 2004

Copyright © Sam Larbie 2002

ISBN 0-9536100-4-7

Printed by Cox & Wyman Ltd, Reading, Berks.

All Scripture quotations are taken from the
NKJV, KJV, and NIV of the Bible,
unless otherwise stated.

Contents

ACKNOWLEDGEMENTS

Writing this book on prayer would not have been possible without the constant reminder, prayer support and encouragement of my dear loving wife Sophie.

Secondly, I have been inspired by the faithful intercessory life of my late father, Elder Emmanuel Kofie Larbie. From 1949, when he received Jesus as his Saviour and Lord, until he died, he was a man of prayer.

I wish also to express my sincere thanks to Alivia Media, Rev Dr Lawrence Tetteh and Mrs Monique Pin, for their immense contribution towards the writing of this book.

I am also very grateful for the support, friendship and unity of the leadership team and members of the Elim Pentecostal Church, Camberwell, and branches. My appreciation also goes to all others who have contributed in diverse ways to the completion of this project.

FOREWORD

There are many people who know how to speak endless words in prayer, but few know how to talk out of their heart to God. Reverend Larbie is one of those few. He does not live by 'regular mealtime' prayers but by healthy portions of intercession, warfare and making his petitions excellently done in the *Awesome Power of Prayer*. His experience as a major in the army has equipped him with a special gift to infiltrate the natural with the spiritual. Reverend Larbie employs the strategies necessary until victory is achieved!

This book is a must read for those wanting a powerful prayer life. Reverend Larbie has certainly given us the 'what' and 'who' of prayer. If applied, we can expect great things from God, getting the results we so much desire.

Dr Kingsley A Fletcher
International speaker, author and pastor,
Research Triangle Park, North Carolina

About the Author

Sam Larbie enlisted in the Ghanaian Army and rose to the rank of major. He commanded an infantry company whilst serving with the United Nations Emergency Force (UNEF) in Egypt and the United Nations Interim Force in Lebanon (UNIFIL) in 1979. He is currently Senior Pastor of the Elim Pentecostal Church, Camberwell, London and has been involved in many major prayer initiatives in England and beyond, including National Prayer Summits. He was the one-time Prayer Chairman of the Annual Mission to London conferences organised by Dr Morris Cerrullo.

Pastor Larbie's ministry is characterised by healing, signs and wonders. He has planted seven churches in London, one in Malmo, Sweden, and six in Ghana. 'The Awesome Power of Prayer' featured as Book of the Month in Direction Magazine and TV4Life Magazine.

Sam is married to Sophie and they have four adult sons who serve the Lord: Thomas, Lawrence, Andrew and David.

INTRODUCTION

The Secretary General of the United Nations, Mr Kofi Annan, long before the outbreak of the first Gulf War, was faced with the daunting task of meeting with the then President Saddam Hussein of Iraq in an attempt to diffuse an impending war between America and Iraq. The whole world hoped for the best as nobody could predict the outcome of this important meeting. Would Kofi Annan be believable before Saddam or would President Hussein see him as a puppet of the West?

I guess the United Nations' General Assembly and the Security Council may have offered counsel to Mr Kofi Annan but at the end of the day, he needed more than human wisdom to accomplish this important task. The fears of the world were allayed when he returned from Baghdad, the capital of Iraq, with the joyous news that, contrary to all expectations, Saddam Hussein had agreed to his proposals. The world heaved a sigh of relief. How did he do it? The impossible had happened!

The media waited anxiously to find out from Kofi Annan how he had achieved the unimaginable. His response was, "Never underrate the *power of prayer*".

I agree very much with this statement. In this book it is my aim to help you appreciate the great power of prayer and how you can channel this power into working for you. I shall also discuss the various forms of prayer.

I shall endeavour to highlight on corporate prayer, which appears to have lost its place in the body of believers these days. I pray that as you read this book you will be brought to the place the Holy Spirit has designed for you to be and that your fellowship will attain greater heights. May the Lord be glorified in your life, your family, your school, your workplace, your community, your nation and the world through your prayers!

CHAPTER ONE

My Prayer Encounter

My first encounter with prayer of a significant measure was when I received a strange letter after I had just been promoted to the rank of a full lieutenant in the Ghanaian Army in 1969.

As I picked up this letter from my pigeonhole, I noticed how odd it was. It had been addressed in pencil and did not have any stamp affixed to the envelope. I sensed that it was a local mail. On opening the envelope I realised that the letter itself was also in pencil and the letters were haphazardly joined together. I tried to read it but I could not make any sense out of it. Then it occurred to me that the letter was in the local language of the area we were in.

I approached a fellow officer to translate the contents for me. After looking carefully at it for some time he said, "Sam, I cannot understand some of the technical language used but I don't think this is good." He then suggested that I showed it to another officer to translate it for me.

The death sentence

By now my anxiety was steadily building up and, to some degree, fear was taking over me. I started to examine who my enemies were among the officers and even the other ranks but could not come up with anyone. I finally reached an officer who read the letter and told me plainly, "This is very bad. You have been given seven days to live." Apparently 'voodoo power' appears to have been invoked against me. This is an invocation of occult power that releases fear in the victim, sometimes leading to a sudden paralysis of the body or sometimes to a lightening strike, resulting in instant death within the period stated.

I had been given seven days to live! I could have dropped dead right there. Apparently, the letter had been written in an occult language. My fears had been real. Immediately my thoughts went to my father who was an elder in a branch of a Pentecostal church in a city, about 25 miles south-east of the military barracks. I was then a platoon commander, and the company of 105 men of which my platoon was a part had been placed on the alert. Therefore we were confined to the barracks for the impending operation. This compounded my predicament, since I could not get away to my father who could help me with prayer against my 'death sentence'. I was quite religious but only prayed occasionally and had never been in this kind of situation before. I lost appetite, skipped my supper and went into my room, holding the damning letter in my hand.

Fear-driven prayer

I locked my door and placed the letter on the centre table, knelt beside it and started to pray. I wished I could pray with other tongues, but I could not. I started gradually but soon gained momentum. There was no one who could help at this time; I was all on my own. I know now that Jesus was with me. I did not feel or experience his presence, but somehow I knew my prayers would not fall on deaf ears.

I lost track of time as the fervency of my prayer picked up. There had been an initial heaviness about the letter on the table, which I could feel around the entire room. As I went on praying, I began to feel lighter and it became easier to pray louder and with more confidence.

I did not realise how long I had been praying, but when I looked at the clock, it was two o'clock in the morning. I had been praying for five-and-a-half hours! There was lightness all around me, I was no longer afraid. I took the letter and placed it back in the envelope. Joy surged inside me. At that moment it dawned on me that Jesus had answered my prayer! I knew it. The venom in the letter had just disappeared. I did not need to worry about going to see my father anymore. Jesus had just done it for me.

I forgot about the letter

Within three days, I had completely forgotten about the letter. But ten days later something dramatic happened.

The first officer I showed the letter to called me and enquired about it. "Which letter?" I asked. "The one you showed me last time," he replied.

I had completely forgotten all about it! Apparently, he had feared that some deadly illness would suddenly grip me and I would die within seven days, as was the usual thing with those kind of occultic 'executions'.

JEREMIAH 33:3

Call to me, and I will answer you...

My prayer had started as a result of my fear of death. Fear is destructive, just as faith is creative. It snow-balls and can quickly cripple you, but faith builds you up. Through the prayer, fear had been overthrown and faith had taken over my being, so that it took somebody to remind me of the evil that I had just escaped.

I had prayed away my fears as I called on Jesus to deal with my enemies and cancel the power of death that had been pronounced over me. I prayed until fear left me and I was free. The two-way communication that prayer incorporates never occurred to me then. If only I had known this, I would have asked the Lord to speak to me. I am sure he would have said a lot, including instruction regarding the future. I said a one-sided prayer but God in his mercy provided an immediate answer.

CHAPTER TWO

What is Prayer and Why Bother?

Could you say this with me?

"Father God, I am not sure whether I understand what prayer is. I am a novice at prayer. I am somewhat hopeless at prayer. In fact, there is so much I do not yet understand about prayer. I am told that prayer is conversation with you. Please teach me the value of prayer, show me how to get to know you better through prayer and, of course, at the same time teach me to pray, and to love to pray.
Amen."

What you have just read is a prayer.
So, what is prayer?

First, it is something very important. That is why the Bible records over 650 prayers. Jesus' disciples asked him to teach them only one thing, and that was to pray. "Lord, teach us to pray" (Luke 11:1).

Jesus' reply was positive: "When you pray, say..." (Luke 11:2). It indicated that Christians are expected to 'pray'. He said 'when' not 'if'.

Secondly, prayer is meant to be powerful and effective.

JAMES 5:16

The effective fervent prayer of a righteous man avails much.

Prayer is essentially relationship with God.

When we pray, we come before God at his initiative and invitation, and the purpose for that invitation is for fellowship (Rev 3:20). That fellowship involves conversing or speaking with God. In that fellowship, we are to come in obedience and submission: kneeling or bowing down (Ps 95:6) in Jewish culture in biblical days signified submission to higher authority (Ezra 9:5).

When you pray, you do so in the knowledge that you must submit to God's will (Job 23:12; Luke 22:41-42). Prayer is God's invitation to discuss any issue he has laid on your heart. Always remember that whatever is on your heart/mind, which you desire to pray about, it is God who caused you to desire to pray about it.

Why should we pray?

This is a legitimate question.

If God knows everything, then why must we bother to pray?

- Jesus expects us to pray. "When you pray, say..." (Luke 11:2). We said earlier any relationship must involve communication. Prayer is the name we give to speaking with God. God is a God of love and we respond in love to his love. He wants us to know him better. Jesus actually gave us a model prayer (Matt 6:9-13, Luke 11:3-4) to pattern our prayers after.

- We are commanded in God's Word to pray, and obedience is vital to Christians (Is 65:24; Jer 33:3; Luke 11:2; Thes 5:16). We can also look at the commandments as an invitation from God for fellowship. In Isaiah 55:6 he invites us to seek him and call upon him.

- Jesus prayed himself whilst he was on earth. Since he is our example, we too must pray. In Luke 2:49, when he was a small boy, Jesus asked his anxious parents: "How is it that you sought me? Did you not know that I must be in my Father's house?" Mark 11:17 explains what his "Father's house" meant. It is the 'house of prayer'.

  You should look at Mark 1:35; Mark 6:45-46; Luke 3:21-22; Luke 5:16; Luke 9:28-29. We are told in Luke 6:12-13 that, on one occasion, he continued in prayer to God all night.

- Jesus prayed for guidance (Luke 6:12-13) so prayer is one sure way by which we can obtain guidance from God.

  Prayer is part of our weaponry of warfare against

Satan (Eph 6:18-19). In prayer, we must always remember that Satan is a defeated foe (Rev 12:7-11 and Col 2:15). As Christians, we battle against the forces of darkness in the victory and strength of the finished work of Jesus on Calvary and in the power of the living Christ.

- This reason is very much linked to the reason above. One aspect of prayer is intercession – standing in the gap for somebody else. Jesus told Simon Peter once: "Simon, Simon, behold, Satan demands to have you, that he might sift you like wheat, but **I have prayed for you** that your faith may not fail" (Luke 22:31-33). Read also Hebrews 5:7. We also are to intercede!

- Prayer is the God-approved way to receive from God what he has prepared for your life. When you ask, you receive and when you knock, you get the door opened for you (John 11:41-44; Matt 7:7).

- Prayer is to be our way of life to the extent that even our last words should be words of prayer. "Father, into thy hands I commit my spirit" were Jesus' last words before he breathed his last (Luke 23:46). Stephen, the first martyr of the Church, prayed, "'Lord, do not hold this sin against them.' After this he died" (Acts 7:54-60).

- The fact that God has stated all these things in his Word should tell us that he is very interested in the prayers of each one of us, no matter how small the issue may be.

What a joy to know that worship was stopped in heaven for half an hour so that the prayers of Christians (including yours) could be heard and answered! (Rev 8:1-5).

- Prayer is God's way of transforming us. Through prayer (Ps 77:16-17) God makes us see as far as he sees, what he sees, how he sees, in the heart he sees.

- Another reason is that God wants us to involve him in the mundane things of our lives. God needs our prayers because he knows we need to know him as he works in our lives. He will only change the world through us and we must be brought to the place where we will know whom we are representing on earth.

- Furthermore, though God is omniscient (all-knowing and the source of all knowledge), omnipotent (all-powerful, almighty), omnipresent (everywhere and anywhere), and all sovereign, he has decided to limit himself by our prayers. He only acts as we pray, since he gave us a responsibility (Gen 2; Ps 8:1-9).

God wants us to pray because he only extends his kingdom through prayer. "Your kingdom come... for yours is the kingdom" (Matt 6:10,13).

"Pray that the Lord of the harvest will send out labourers into the field" (Matt 9:38).

We pray to prove for ourselves that God's Word and promises are indeed true. When we pray we expect to be answered. Every answer to prayer is a present-day testimony to God's faithfulness. This helps our own faith and through our testimony, others are encouraged to pray.

Let me give you some homework. As you read your Bible and as you pray, get a notebook and continue to add to the above-mentioned reasons on why you must pray.

PRAYER

Father God, I have just read about a number of reasons why I should pray. Convince me more of each of the above reasons and give me more reasons in my life as I embark on a prayer journey with you. Thank you. Amen!

CHAPTER THREE

Forms of Prayer 1: ACTS

When you magnify the omnipotence of God, you will be placing yourself in a position to see the Lord in his true magnificence. Immediately you will see yourself, your needs and problems in their right perspective. After the adoration (Isaiah 40:12-26), listen to what the Lord says: In the sixth chapter of the gospel of Matthew, Jesus teaches his disciples how to pray.

MATTHEW 6:9-13

In this manner, therefore, pray:

Our Father in heaven,
Hallowed be your name.
Your kingdom come.
Your will be done
On earth as it is in heaven.
Give us this day our daily bread.
And forgive us our debts,
As we forgive our debtors.
And do not lead us into temptation,

But deliver us from the evil one.
For yours is the kingdom and the power
And the glory forever. Amen.

I believe that the prayer he taught them, which we call 'The Lord's Prayer', is really the pattern that all prayer must follow. This means that at any time we pray, we need to pray according to the principles outlined in that prayer. Over the years, I have come to the realisation that the best way to learn how to pray is to pray. You can hardly be taught how to pray without praying. That is why when his disciples asked him to teach them how to pray, Jesus said to them, "In this manner, therefore, pray..." (Matthew 6:9).

Pattern for prayer

In The Lord's Prayer, is there a pattern? Are there principles to follow? These are legitimate questions many ask. The answer to both questions is 'yes'.

In teaching his disciples to pray, Jesus starts with adoration: "Our Father in heaven, hallowed be your name. Your kingdom come. Your will be done on earth as it is in heaven."

This is followed by supplication (a humble request for help): "Give us this day our daily bread... and do not lead us into temptation, but deliver us from the evil one."

Then there is confession: "And forgive us our debts..."

Finally there is thanksgiving: "For yours is the kingdom and the power and the glory forever. Amen."

In order to make it easy to remember, let us use the acronym, **ACTS**: **A**doration, **C**onfession, **T**hanksgiving and **S**upplication.

Adoration

To adore somebody is to exalt the person and give the person his/her worth. Adoration is simply appreciating vocally the good things about someone. It is the same as praise. God is so good that he has given us a manual for praise. The Psalms are full of praise and give us a basis to learn to use our own words in praise as the psalmists do. In Psalm 104:1, we read:

Bless the Lord, O my soul! O Lord my God, you are very great: you are clothed with honour and majesty.

Adoration is our response to two questions: Who is God? (What is his character and nature?) And what is God like? (What are his attributes?)

Thanksgiving is different: we thank God for what he has done!

Just open your mouth and speak aloud to God with meaning what you know about who he is and his attributes. Adoration and praise is not just saying or shouting, "I adore you, Lord! I bless you, Lord! I praise you, Lord! I magnify you! I exalt you, Lord! I love you and I extol you, Lord." Yes, these are good and you may say these words from the depths of your heart, but they are not enough. Go further! Let us look at The Lord's Prayer – the model prayer. "Our Father... hallowed be your name." What does it mean to hallow the name of

God? It means honouring God's name (character and attitudes). It is appreciating him for who he is.

How do we go about adoring God?

Let me recommend a simple guide, which can be derived from The Lord's Prayer. It is this:

We adore God for...

(i) his Fatherhood	('Our Father...')
(ii) his eternity	('...who is in heaven...')
(iii) his holiness	('...hallowed be your name.')
(iv) his love	('Our Father...' and 'Your kingdom come. Your will be done on earth as it is in heaven.')
	God so loved the world that Jesus came to destroy Satan's kingdom and usher in God's kingdom.
(v) his power	('For yours is the kingdom and the power and the glory forever.')

To adore God is to publicly 'boast' about the character of God and magnify his name. This could develop into singing his praises. Praises in prayer could be in the form of speaking or singing. It should not be a mechanical or casual repetition of adjectives, but a true affirmation of admiration and worship that comes out of a proper recognition of who he is and the value you place on him. Try asking yourself some questions about what the Lord means to you.

(i) Adoring God for his fatherhood

There are two aspects to his fatherhood. First, he is the Father of all creation.

The second aspect is the more glorious. He is the Father of all those who receive Jesus Christ as Saviour (John 1:12). Appreciate God for his gift of his Son!

As our Father, God protects us and cares for our needs. This attribute is more relevant when it comes to thanksgiving. God is the Father who is totally dependable, very caring and trustworthy. He is completely and utterly faithful and just in all his ways. To him alone is all honour and reverence. He wants us to petition him, to direct our needs and wants to him, calling on him day and night.

Just begin to appreciate the fatherhood now. Take a look at your own body and see how perfect and unique your features are. These thoughts make you see how awesome the Lord is.

PSALM 8:4-9

What is man that you are mindful of him? And the son of man that you visit him? For you have made him a little lower than the angels, and you have crowned him with glory and honour. You have made him to have dominion over the works of your hands; you have put all things under his feet... O Lord, our Lord, how excellent is your name in all the earth!

(ii) Adoring God for his eternity

The next thing you must focus on when adoring the Lord is his eternity. He has no beginning and no end. He cannot be confined to time and space. This also means he is omnipresent, omniscient and omnipotent. The best way to adore his eternity is to adore his omniscience and his omnipresence.

Adoring the Lord who is omniscient

JEREMIAH 1:5

Before I formed you in the womb I knew you; and before you were born I sanctified you...

PSALM 139:2-4

You know my sitting down and my rising up; you understand my thought afar off. You comprehend my path and my lying down, and are acquainted with all my ways. For there is not a word on my tongue, but behold, O Lord, you know it altogether.

This description of God details the part of his personality that knows and understands all things. Every mystery is wrapped up in him. God knows the end from the beginning. He knows everything about everything. Before you were formed in your mother's womb, he knew you and called you by name. No matter where your mother met your father, God already knew you. To know that this is the kind of God we are praying to, it makes me feel good. It makes me feel that my words are not falling on deaf ears. I am assured that my prayers are going to the right place, to that Person who knows me better than I even know myself.

Adoring the Lord who is omnipresent God

His omniscience and eternity makes him omnipresent.

MATTHEW 28:20

...Lo, I am with you always, even to the end of the age. Amen.

PSALM 139:8-13

If I ascend into heaven, you are there: if I make my bed in hell, behold, you are there. If I take the wings of the morning, and dwell in the uttermost parts of the sea; even there your hand shall lead me, and your right hand shall hold me. If I say, "Surely the darkness shall fall on me," even the night shall be light about me. Indeed the darkness shall not hide from you; but the night shines as the day; the darkness and the light are both alike to you. For you formed my inward parts; you covered me in my mother's womb.

God is also omnipresent. That means he is everywhere at every time. That is why you can be in London and pray concerning somebody or something in Africa. Sometimes I pray for people over the phone and they receive the answer they desired. Am I saying that God is travelling on the airwaves? No! He is already there. He is omnipresent, but the devil is localised.

The devil is limited. When Jesus was on planet Earth, he was also localised because he couldn't be in two places at the same time. But since he was raised by God, he is everywhere. So wherever you are, you can pray and it will be effective. There are some folks who think that you cannot pray when you are in the toilet or any such place, as if God shuns the toilet because it is not 'holy'. Jesus is there with you, wherever you may be.

You don't have to pray in a special language, as some people believe. There are some Christians who think that God answers prayer more quickly only when you speak with special languages like Hebrew or Latin. Please don't let us make the Lord into something that he is not. He listens to any cry and answers to any language. Do not forget that he created English, French, Spanish and all the other languages! Also know that we do not need any special accent for God to hear us.

Your faith will become strong as you have this knowledge, that God is present everywhere, so that it doesn't matter if you sit, stand, lie or kneel when praying. He hears it anyhow. As a matter of fact, even if you shout the name 'Jesus' accidentally or unconsciously, he hears.

(iii) Adoring God for his holiness

Hallowed be your name.

One attribute of God is his holiness. Without holiness no one can see God. Holiness means uniqueness, separateness.

1 SAMUEL 2:2

"There is none holy like the Lord, there is none besides our God."

Boast about the holiness of God!

(iv) Adoring God for his love

Jesus is the embodiment of God's love for us. He died to bring us back to God! So praise God for the death and resurrection of Jesus.

He has established a new kingdom. So when Jesus teaches his disciples to pray: "Your kingdom come. Your will be done..." it is in praise of the work Jesus came to start which is being continued by the Holy Spirit.

Let me narrate a story to show the power in the name of Jesus.

This story was told of a man whose vehicle broke down in the middle of a narrow bridge that only allowed one car to pass at a time. As he stood contemplating on what to do, he saw a huge truck coming at him. Then he saw a woman going across the road behind his car and he knew that he could not escape from being hit by the oncoming truck, and neither would the woman. In his confusion, he shouted, "Jesus!" To his surprise the truck made it safely past his car and missed the woman at the same time. It was incredible! The man testified that he could not account for what happened. He believed that the Lord sent angels to stretch the bridge. By just scream-ing the name 'Jesus', the Lord who is omnipresent heard him. Wherever you are, call on him and he will hear you.

The Bible reveals several names and titles of Jesus. Look for these and begin to boast about them in adoration.

Take time to appreciate and acknowledge the names of God. Since Jesus is the express image of the Father (Heb 1:3) and also God (Joel 1:1). You can actually take the names of Jesus and just praise him.

You can go through the alphabet, listing his names:

A He is **A**lmighty, **A**lpha and Omega,
and our **A**dvocate.

B He is the **B**read of life, **B**read from
heaven.

C He is the **C**reator. He is our **C**ounsellor.
He is **C**hrist (anointed to bring liberty
and redemption).

D He is our **D**eliverer.

E He is **E**xalted. He is the **E**ternal God.

F He is our **F**riend. He is **F**aithful.

G He is **G**reat. He is **G**od. He is **G**ood.
He is **G**lorious.

H He is **H**oly. He is **H**onourable.
He is the **H**ealer.

I He is our **I**ntercessor. He is **I**mmortal.
He is **I**ncomparable.

J He is our **J**udge. He is the **J**ust one who
Justifies the unjust.

K He is **K**ing of kings. He is **K**nowledgeable.

L He is **L**ord of lords. He is **L**ove.

M He is **M**an of War. He is the **M**aster.

N His **N**ame is above all names.
He is our **N**ourisher.

O He is the **O**bedient **O**ne. **O**mnipotent God.

P He is the **P**rince of **P**eace.
   He is our High **P**riest. He is **P**erfect.

Q He is always **Q**uick, he is never late.

R He is the **R**uler. He is **R**ighteous.
   He is our **R**esurrection.

S He is our **S**hepherd. He is **S**overeign.

T He is the **T**rustworthy One.
   He is our **T**eacher.

U He is **U**nderstanding. He **U**pholds all
   things by the word of his **P**ower.
   He is **U**nequalled. He is **U**nconquerable.

V He is the true **V**ine. **V**engeance belongs
   to him. He is always **V**ictorious.

W He is **W**orthy. He is **W**isdom and all
   Wise. His **W**rath goes out against sin.
   He is **W**ealth. He is the **W**ealth of the
   nations.

X He is **X**cellent!

Y He is **Y**eshua (Hebrew word for Jesus).
   He is **Y**ahweh!

Z He is the **Z**enith of our hope. He is '**Z**oë'
   (the Greek word for eternal life).

Take each of these and think about it. Ask God to help you appreciate the name or attribute to inspire you to praise as a result. Do not wait until you feel like praising. Feeling is in the flesh and the devil will not want you to feel like praising his enemy. Just believe that God is inspiring you in answer to prayer. It is his will that you praise him.

(v) Adoring God for his power

Adoring the omnipotent God

This derives from "For yours is the kingdom and the power and the glory..."

When doing this, your focus must be on the supremacy and unending power of the Lord. A close look at planet Earth fills one with wonder and admiration. It is like a pumpkin, slightly flattened at the top and the bottom. What is it that holds everything together and in place? This power is known as gravity. Should it fail everything will fall into space. Who keeps this gravity active at all times? The sun does not fall on us and neither does the sea engulf us. This is the omnipotence of the Lord. It has been suggested by scientists that if the sun were just a little closer to our planet, its rays would burn up the earth, and if it were just a little further away, then everything on earth would freeze because nothing would escape from the bitter cold that would result. Remember also that there are other known planets – Mars, Venus, Mercury, Jupiter, Uranus, Neptune, Saturn and Pluto. And we are discovering other astral bodies besides these planets all the time. They do not crash into one another. They stay out there in their places in space. What an amazing and powerful Creator!

PSALM 19:1-6

The heavens declare the glory of God; And the firmament shows his handiwork. Day unto day utters speech, and night unto night reveals knowledge. There is no speech or language, where their voice is not heard. Their line has gone out through all the earth, and their words to the end of the world. In them, he has set a tabernacle for the sun, which is like a bridegroom coming out of his chamber, and rejoices like a strong man to run its race. Its rising is from one end of heaven, and its circuit to the other end; and there is nothing hidden from its heat.

ISAIAH 40:12-17

Who has measured the waters in the hollow of his hands, measured heaven with a span, and calculated the dust of the earth in a measure, weighed the mountains in scales, and the hills in a balance? Who has directed the Spirit of the LORD, *or as his counsellor has taught him? With whom did he take counsel, and who instructed him, and taught him in the path of justice? Who taught him knowledge, and showed him the way of understanding? Behold, the nations are as a drop in a bucket, and are counted as the small dust on the scales; look, he lifts up the isles as a very little thing. And Lebanon is not sufficient to burn, nor its beasts sufficient for a burnt offering. All nations before him are as nothing; and they are counted by him less than nothing, and worthless.*

ISAIAH 40:22-23; 25-26

It is he who sits above the circle of the earth, and its inhabitants are like grasshoppers; who stretches out the heavens like a curtain, and spreads them out like a tent to dwell in: he brings the princes to nothing: he makes the judges of the earth useless... "To whom then will you liken me, or to whom shall I be equal?" says the Holy One. Lift up your eyes on high, and see who has created these things, who brings out their host by number: he calls them all by name by the greatness of his might, and the strength of his power; not one is missing.

Is it not wonderful that this great God who created the whole universe is interested in you and me? When you start thinking about this, you will begin to magnify God. Any time you magnify anything, you are not making it any bigger than it already is. It is more about the way you see it – you will be seeing it bigger than you would normally have seen it. It is like using a magnifying glass to read something. The characters are enlarged but the subject does not change. It is your vision that is changed so that you see the object in greater detail and with better understanding.

So when you magnify the omnipotence of God, you are placing yourself in a position to see the Lord in his true magnificence. As a result, you will see yourself, your needs and problems in their right perspective. After the adoration (Isaiah 40:12-26 above), listen to what the Lord says:

ISAIAH 40:27-31

Why do you say, O Jacob, and speak, O Israel: "My way is hidden from the LORD, and my just claim is passed over by my God"? Have you not known? Have you not heard? The everlasting God, the LORD, the Creator of the ends of the earth, neither faints nor is weary. His understanding is unsearchable. He gives power to the weak, and to those who have no might he increases strength. Even the youths shall faint and be weary, and the young men shall utterly fall: but those who wait on the LORD shall renew their strength; they shall mount up with wings like eagles; they shall run, and not be weary; they shall walk and, not faint.

Is that not that wonderful? That is the result of adoration.

Confession

Arising out of our praise to God for his holiness, we need to confess our sins. Before we bring our requests to God, we need to clear any 'debts' based on God's Word. Psalm 66:18 states, "If I regard iniquity in my heart, the Lord will not hear me."

To confess your sin is to open your heart to God and say, "God, I am sorry".

In confession you must be honest about the sins you have committed and genuinely ask the Lord for his forgiveness. It requires calling the sins by name, one after the other, and not merely generalising casually. Often we bunch everything up and ask God for forgiveness of our sins in order to satisfy this requirement of prayer. We say, "Lord, forgive me for where I have gone wrong." It is important that you sincerely acknowledge any particular sin that you are aware of and ask for and receive the Lord's forgiveness.

God knows everything about us. He is omniscient, but God has created human beings with a will. God respects our right to free choice.

You have to be willing to accept God's decision that what he says is wrong against him is wrong. It is he who convicts us of sin (John 16:12). When the Holy Spirit convicts us it is for our freedom.

The psalmist's prayer should be our prayer as we come to this stage! "Search me, O God and know my heart. Try me and know my thoughts. And see if there be any hurtful way in me..." (Ps 139:23,24).

Sin is a rejection of the Father's love. He sees the state of your heart far more than you can see it. Allow him to deal with the pride in your heart so that his forgiveness and mercy shall come to you. As you submit your heart to him, he will show you the sins that you may not have been aware of.

During this phase of prayer it is important:

(a) to wait for the Holy Spirit to convict you. Take a pen and paper and write down the things the Holy Spirit brings to memory, the things that you have done wrong against God. Be careful that you do not allow the enemy to accuse you!

(b) to remember that God must show you how he sees you, and that you must see yourself as God sees you. Our duty as Christians here is again to "be still" – let go and allow God to do the searching; you are co-labourers with God (1 Cor 6:1).

So you are to cooperate actively with the blessed Holy Spirit, the third person of the blessed Trinity, in whatever he is doing in you and with you.

(c) that confession starts when you willingly agree to stop resisting the Holy Spirit's search of your heart (Ps 139:23,24) and agree to see your life, your attitudes, your thoughts, your words, your actions and inactions in God's way. As you focus on the Saviour and what your sins cost him, you begin to feel shame for your sins, and as you trust him for forgiveness, you must resolve not to commit those sins again by the strength of the Holy Spirit.

PSALM 32:5-6

I acknowledged my sin to you, and my iniquity I have not hidden. I said, "I will confess my transgressions to the LORD," and you forgave the iniquity of my sin. For this cause everyone who is godly shall pray to you in a time when you may be found...

There are times when you may find it hard to forgive yourself. You feel too ashamed and sorry that you have succumbed to whatever sin you may have committed. Please hold it right there! The sin was first against the Lord before yourself, so stop misplacing the order and go right now to the Lord and ask for forgiveness for the original sin and the sin of pride that has now overtaken your heart.

LUKE 15:18

I will arise and go to my father, and will say to him, "Father, I have sinned against heaven and before you."

(d) Receive God's forgiveness with gratitude. He is a merciful God and willing to cleanse you of all unrighteousness. After you confess your sin(s), ask him for forgiveness and believe that he is granting it. Forgiveness is his promise to us if we confess our sins; claim it and believe that you have it and it shall be yours (1 John 1:9).

The two extremes

Always remember that your sins are first against the Father, who is more important than you. So when he forgives you, you have no justification to punish yourself any longer. Sin-consciousness is one of the major problems to deal with when it comes to confessions. While the haughty in spirit has an uncaring attitude about his sins, the sin-conscious person is also at the other extreme and cannot believe that he is worthy to be forgiven. But the Word of God should be taken for what it says.

Some people are driven into frustration and apathy and blame themselves for unanswered prayer. They believe that the reason they're not receiving answers to their requests is because of some unconfessed sin in their lives. Therefore, the only prayer they make is, "Lord forgive me, Lord forgive me".

The condition for forgiveness

The Word of the Lord is always true and there is no other meaning to what it says than just what it says:

1 JOHN 1:9

"If we confess our sins, he is faithful and just to forgive us our sins, and to cleanse us from all unrighteousness."

Take note that this promise of forgiveness and cleansing comes with a condition. "If we confess our sins..." We must perform the act of identifying the sin and going before him, believing that he will do what he has promised to do. His condition is not difficult. All the Lord is asking of you is that you will acknowledge your sin by name, and then the blood of Jesus will immediately go into action to effect a total cleansing. It becomes a matter of course once the conditions are right.

Self-pity does not help

Some people wallow in self-pity, feeling sorry for themselves and thinking that if the Lord sees how much they beat themselves he will forgive them and take away the burden of sin they have been feeling. Do not allow the devil to deceive you. Self-pity does not get you anything; it instead takes you away from the forgiveness you desire.

Such people do not see themselves in the Word of God and do not believe they merit the Lord's forgiveness. We do not work for the Lord's blessings. We receive them by grace – undeserved love and forgiveness. Stop condemning yourself, turn to Calvary and allow the blood that Jesus shed, that flows from the cross, to cleanse you and make you free.

Bob Forster

I remember a story an old friend told me. There was a man called Bob Forster who suffered from a mental disorder and was in an institution. His problem was that he believed he was a piece of grain and was afraid that any chicken could eat him up. Whenever he was asked, "Bob, who are you?" he would answer, "a piece of grain". Bob Forster stayed in the psychiatric hospital for a considerable period of time until the authorities believed he had been cured and no longer thought of himself as a piece of grain. He was discharged and handed over to his relatives.

On the way home they had to walk across a field to catch a train. As they walked Bob Forster stopped abruptly, to the surprise of everyone. There was a cockerel pacing about on the field. Bob looked at it fixedly and asked, "Does it know that I am Bob Forster and not a piece of grain?" They instantly made a u-turn to the hospital because Bob's perception of himself had not changed. Even though he said with his mouth that he was Bob Forster, his heart did not believe it. God hates proud and haughty people. The Bible says he resists them. God resists the proud but gives grace to the humble (1 Peter 5:5). It must be pride, abject ignorance or total delusion that will make you think that you have no sin to confess.

1 JOHN 1:8

If we say we have no sin, we deceive ourselves, and the truth is not in us.

Thanksgiving

To thank God is to show gratitude for what he has done.

PSALM 100:4

Enter into his gates with thanksgiving, and into his courts with praise: be thankful unto him, and bless his name.

We owe the Lord thanks for giving us Jesus Christ, his only begotten Son, who in turn gave up his life on the cross for us. He became our link to God. He deserves thanksgiving. But for his death on the cross, sin would still have had dominion over us. Through his death we have our redemption.

ROMANS 3:24-26

...Being justified freely by his grace through the redemption that is in Christ Jesus: whom God set forth as a propitiation by his blood through faith, to demonstrate his righteousness, because in his forbearance God had passed over the sins that were previously committed, to demonstrate at the present time his righteousness: that he might be just, and the justifier of the one who has faith in Jesus.

I believe that this great sacrifice and transformation the Lord has brought into our lives is reason

41

enough for us to give him thanks, always and eternally.

Jesus took upon himself every accusation of the devil against us on the cross. It is therefore no wonder that he cried out, "My God, my God, why have you forsaken me?" There was no response from the Father because Jesus at that time carried the sins of humanity on himself. He had become sin. He is worthy to be thanked, praised and adored.

The wilderness mentality

When you are thankful you must demonstrate your gratitude through your actions. Some people are so ungrateful that their attitude stinks. When the Lord does anything for them they act as if nothing has happened, and it is then that they even complain about the things they have not got yet. This is what I call the 'wilderness mentality'.

The Israelites had been in tortuous slavery in Egypt, where they were treated ruthlessly and viciously. For many years they cried unto the Lord to deliver them from oppression. God heard them and sent Moses to come and lead them to the land that he had prepared for them. The journey to the promised land was through a wilderness. God performed several dramatic miracles for them, from Egypt to the wilderness, including raining down their daily supply of food. After some time they started complaining and even wished that they were back in Egypt. Oh, what ingratitude!

Then the whole congregation of the children of Israel complained against Moses and Aaron in the wilderness.

And the children of Israel said to them:

EXODUS 16:2-3

"Oh, that we have died by the hand of the LORD in the land of Egypt, when we sat by the pot of meat and when we ate bread to the full! For you have brought us into this wilderness to kill this whole assembly with hunger."

Any time we are not thankful we are just saying, like the Israelites in the wilderness, that we were better off without his help and wish that we were back where we were before he helped us. Even we as human beings get hurt when we are not thanked for the gifts we give.

According to Ghanaian tradition, when someone gives you a gift or does something for you, you are expected to go and say thank you before sunrise the next day. They will be expecting it and your reputation and prospect of ever getting anything again depends on it.

God also desires thanksgiving. In Luke Chapter 17, ten lepers came to ask Jesus to heal them and he asked them to go and show themselves to the priests. As they went on their way, they were healed but only one came back to thank him.

This event was so significant that it was recorded as well as Jesus' disapproval of the nine who failed to come back:

LUKE 17:17

So Jesus answered and said, "Were there not ten cleansed? But where are the nine?"

When you get to understand the importance of saying thanks to the Lord, you will not be shy to stand before his congregation to say thanks for the job, the child, the money, etc, that he gave you. When you give thanks, it is a sign that you remember through whose assistance you came by your blessing. Thanksgiving is so important to God that numerous times throughout the Bible he elaborates the various blessings he has given to us and cautions us never to forget it.

PSALM 103:1-2

Bless the LORD, O my soul: and all that is within me bless his holy name. Bless the LORD, O my soul: and forget not all his benefits.

DEUTERONOMY 8:18

And you shall remember the LORD your God: for it is he who gives you power to get wealth...

PSALM 118:1

Oh, give thanks to the LORD; for he is good: for his mercy endures for ever.

Do not be only grateful inwardly. Express your gratitude outwardly. The Lord deserves it!

Supplication

Supplication means to make a humble request, to plead or seek humbly. The Amplified Bible defines supplication as to petition or to make requests. It means to place your needs before the Lord and to ask for his help.

PHILIPPIANS 4:6

Be anxious for nothing; but in every thing by prayer and supplication with thanksgiving let your requests be made known to God.

Supplication is not limited to personal needs only, but it can also be made for all categories of needs from individuals to nations. Petitioning or supplicating requires dedication and seriousness. It demands focus and avoidance of distractions. You will have to be committed, serious and have a burning desire to see that particular need met. It may necessitate your becoming tired, hungry and ashamed.

Above all, supplication shows your faith in the Lord, that even if he may not answer instantly, he will do so eventually. Jesus gives us a classic description of this form of prayer with a parable in Luke Chapter 18.

LUKE 18:1-8

Then he spoke a parable to them, that men always ought to pray and not lose heart, saying: "There was in a certain city a judge who did not fear God nor regard man. Now there was a widow in that city and she came to him,

45

saying, "Get justice for me from my adversary." And he would not for a while: but afterward he said within himself, "Though I do not fear God, nor regard man, yet because this widow troubles me, I will avenge her, lest by her continual coming she weary me." Then the Lord said, "Hear what the unjust judge said." And shall God not avenge his own elect, who cry out day and night to him, though he bears long with them? I tell you that he will avenge them speedily. Nevertheless when the Son of man comes, will he really find faith on the earth?

It is important that you make prayer a habit; otherwise it will become a tedious ritual, which will be unfulfilling and unprofitable for you. The book of Luke recalls several times that Jesus prayed, from his baptism to his final words on the cross.

He would often withdraw from everyone and enter into communion with his Father. His relationship with his heavenly Father thrived on constant contact and communication. Such was the success of their regular communication that Jesus declared, "I and my Father are one" (John 10:30). The regular flow of information between each of them ensured that the relationship was active and alive. Out of this relationship came Jesus' power.

JOHN 14:10

...The words that I speak to you I do not speak on my own authority; but the Father who dwells in me does the works.

A prayer life that is only propelled by need is temporary. If you are only driven by occasion to seriously pray, you will not build any consistency in prayer. Relationships are not built on occasional contact. Any such association is not deep and will not last long. Always remember that God's interaction with us is according to grace, which only comes out of relationship. So let us aim at building a relationship with him rather than treating him like a spare tyre that we only go for when we are in need.

Often, due to the pressures of the need, some Christians even embark on a fast. Is it possible to twist God's arm or hoodwink him into giving you what you need? There are many instances when there is a delay or the answer does not come. Then some people start looking around for somebody to intercede for them.

The urgency of the need may also cause you to 'open fire' immediately you get on your knees, and one after the other you pour out your requests. There is no thought at all given to the fact that God may want to say something to you right then. We must learn to honour and revere God. Let us do this first before we bring our 'shopping list'. That is why, whenever we pray, we must always remember to start with *praise and thanksgiving!*

CHAPTER FOUR

Forms of Prayer 2: Shopping Lists

Prayer can be described as a personal communication or petition addressed to God in the form of **A**doration, **C**onfession, **T**hanksgiving and **S**upplication. Supplication is the making of requests, which I choose to call 'shopping lists'. In this chapter I intend to take you through the various types of shopping lists and their importance or areas of effectiveness.

Prayer requests are crucial, because they serve as indicators to determine whether we shall receive answers or not. Your requests also show the level of your maturity on the spiritual to carnal scale. The book of James tells us that because of the requests that are made, some prayers do not get answered.

JAMES 4:3

You ask and do not receive, because you ask amiss, that you may spend it on your pleasures.

Prayers that are generated by needs are varied. The needs could be material, emotional or spiritual. Each individual's order of priority is according to his level of understanding of the Word of God and its perceived effect on their lives. For most Christians, the time spent on each need is determined by these same reasons. The fact that you cry and hurt is not what moves the Lord to your assistance. It is so easy to take refuge in your emotion and expect the Lord to be taken in also. Actually, you are better off spending time with the Word of God so that you can find out the best way to approach him with your problem.

I believe that in as much as God will want you to receive all the material things that you want, he has a preferred way for you to receive it.

MATTHEW 6:33

But seek first the kingdom of God, and his righteousness and all these things shall be added to you.

What is the Lord asking of us by this command? We should in all things, including prayer, focus on the needs of God first. Our priority in life must reflect our priorities in prayer. Eternal things are of more consequence than earthly pleasures. The joy of supplication is found when we practically supplicate according to the acronym **JOY**, in obedience to Matthew 6:33.

We should pray firstly for the needs of **J**esus, secondly for the needs of **O**thers and finally for the needs of **Y**ourself.

Therefore, in this chapter, I will not teach you how to pray for the Lord to give you a new car, but I will show you how you could pray for needs that have a more eternal blend.

What are the needs of Jesus?
To answer is simple: the kingdom of God.

1   Leadership of the Church

PROVERBS 29:18

Where there is no revelation, the people cast off restraint...

Wherever there are leaders, there should be vision. But whenever there is no vision, the people perish. Visions create a path for leaders, and as they walk on this path others follow. So whenever these paths are not there, the people find it difficult to locate their destination. It is just like going to a place you have never been to before. When you are left alone you may not find your way home and this can lead to a state of despair.

And the result of despair and confusion is often destruction. When the Israelites left Egypt and were chased by Pharaoh and his army, they came to the Red Sea, an obstacle they had not anticipated, and they were terrified. This caused them to protest and criticise Moses their leader, who was equally confused. Thankfully, he sought God, who told him to strike the sea with his rod.

Instantly, the sea divided, making a way for them to cross. Imagine what would have happened to the whole nation of Israel and God's plan for the future salvation of humanity if Moses had been overtaken by his fear and not called on God at the time he did.

1 TIMOTHY 2:1-2

Therefore, I exhort first of all that supplications, prayers, intercessions, and giving of thanks, be made for all men; for kings, and all who are in authority, that we may lead a quiet and peaceable life in all godliness and reverence.

God's plan is that followers will pray for leaders so that their leaders would see their way clearly, then they will lead them into life and not destruction. We ought to pray for our leaders to evolve policies that run with the Word of God and not otherwise. Then we will have pastors who will not be afraid to rebuke, correct and reprove with the Word when necessary. The standard of the Gospel cannot be compromised in any way by the weakness of any man. It is men who must organise their lives to follow after God's instructions in his Word and not the other way round.

One important thing about leadership is that it is not easy to lead people. People have wrong attitudes, which are brought to the church, and the leader has to help them find the right way to live. This often results in a tug of war with the pastors. However, the one who prays for his leaders is not only obeying Scripture but also curing himself of the naturally wrong attitudes against the man of God. Your prayer support eases the hurt and pain that many of God's men and women go through everyday.

Furthermore, according to 1 Timothy, it is beneficial for us to pray for those in authority, for then we will "lead a quiet and peaceable life in all godliness and honesty." Having our peace in the nation, community and church is directly linked and dependent on our prayers for our leaders. This is the Word of God!

2 Pray for the Christian workers

(LUKE 10:2)

..."The harvest is plentiful, but the labourers are few. Pray therefore the Lord of the harvest to send out labourers into the harvest."

In addition to praying for your church leaders, it is important to include other churches, ministries and missionaries you know, on your prayer list.

Pray, for example, that God will protect them and raise them up in line with his Word in Ephesians 4:11-16.

3 Superiors and kings

1 TIMOTHY 2:1-2

...Supplications, prayers, intercessions, and giving of thanks, be made for all men, for kings, and all who are in authority...

Another category of people we are called to pray for is those over us in the secular world. The Lord recognises that some of our supervisors and bosses can be cantankerous and unreasonable, so he has set in place a solution by which his people can prevail over that. God's design is that we will enjoy peace and quietness and this comes through our prayer.

Probably the problem you are having with your superior is as a result of something you are doing wrongly. Fortunately the Lord knows us through and through, so he works on your heart as you pray for your superior thereby reforming your attitude. As you pray, you will be surprised by the extent of unforgiveness and bitterness embedded in your heart. By God's grace there is healing for you as you obey and pray for your superior.

4   Offenders

MATTHEW 5:44

...Pray for those who spitefully use you and persecute you.

For so long as you are alive in this world, people will offend you. Therefore, in order for us not to be bound by these offences, God has given us the ability and capacity to deal with it – prayer! If there is someone who has been a pest to you, start praying for him or her. Begin investing into your deliverance from their annoyance.

5   Your non-Christian friends

Pray that the veil will fall from their eyes (2 Cor 4:3-4) and they will open their heart willingly to God (John 7:17, Acts 16:14).

6   Immediate family

Pray for their salvation.

Acts 16:31 states "...Believe in the Lord Jesus, and you will be saved – you and your household," claiming this promise. Pray the same prayer you pray for your non-Christian friends.

JAMES 5:16

...And pray for one another, that you may be healed. The effective, fervent prayer of a righteous man avails much.

As a parent, you must use your parental authority to invoke God's blessing on your children. God has entrusted you with his gift of children (Psalm 127:3-5). Your elevation to fatherhood and motherhood came from God. Consequently, you have a right to go to him to ask for a blessing for that which he gave you.

This is what the Lord says about the gift he has given to you:

PROVERBS 10:22

The blessing of the LORD makes one rich, and he adds no sorrow with it.

So if you notice any blemish on the gift, go to him and he will fix it.

A spouse is also a blessing:

PROVERBS 18:22

He who finds a wife finds a good thing, and obtains favour from the LORD.

A wife is like a deep well, with great attributes, and the praying husband will bring them out of her. As you go on your knees to pray for your wife, the best qualities in her come forth and she is transformed into the virtuous woman in Proverb 31. Like precious minerals deeply entrenched in the ground, it takes time, determination, consistency and patience to excavate, but when you lay hands on it, the joy it brings makes nonsense of the effort it took to get it. Likewise, with enduring prayer and love you will find the treasure stored in your spouse. Wives must also pray for their husbands. Children must pray for their parents.

7 National issues

PSALM 9:17

The wicked shall be turned into hell, and all the nations that forget God.

Fellow Christian, the destiny of your nation depends on you. There are issues weighing down on your country that can only change through divine intervention, because they have spiritual origins. All across the world, nations are going through economic crises, military upheavals, social degradation and many more ills, but the Lord says:

2 CHRONICLES 7:14

If my people, who are called by my name, will humble themselves, and pray, and seek my face... then will I hear from heaven... and heal their land.

8   International issues

GENESIS 26:4

...I will give to your descendants all these lands; and in your seed all the nations of the earth shall be blessed...

We hold the key to arresting the rot that is taking over our world. Through the advancement in technology every part of the world has become easily accessible. It has therefore become much easier for deprivation to move across borders from country to country. There is no secular establishment that can cure this world of its sicknesses, but through the Church and us, all the nations of the earth shall be blessed.

9   ...and finally pray for yourself

CHAPTER FIVE

Forms of Prayer 3: Expentancy and Hearing from God

We have said that prayer is a personal communication between you and God. It is a two-way conversation. You talk to God and God responds.

Prayer can become routine and mechanical. You could easily go through the ACTS formula and then rush out when you finish praying.

When we pray, we send messages to God and we must expect to hear from him. It is a dialogue and not a monologue. Many Christians just walk away as if there is no feedback from God. But our God is not like that, he loves us and desires to have fellowship with us. He may even want to chat with you, and all this is possible through the five senses he gave us to relate with this physical world. We have the senses of sight, smell, touch, hearing and taste.

Ignorant people label a person who loses these senses a 'vegetable'. This is the same in the spiritual.

You become like a 'vegetable' when your senses become dead in relation to the Lord. God uses our five senses to communicate with us. It might surprise you that even though faith operates outside the areas of the five senses, God can speak to his children through the medium of their senses. Therefore, all the senses are important because through them God releases spiritual things to us.

We hear from three sources: God, Satan and ourselves. When God speaks, it comes to pass because he is God. When a person hears from himself, he may think he is hearing from God and prophesy. But such prophesies never come to pass. The other source is Satan. He also uses the five senses to send all kinds of messages.

We need to have information for our prayer to be effective. God always speaks. He speaks through his Word and he also speaks through the Holy Spirit.

The sense of sight – the 'eye gate'

Through the eyes we have a framework for visions, dreams and trances. I will relate them to Scripture so that you can properly identify and understand the particular thing that the Holy Spirit may be revealing to you.

Visions
(a) Closed-eye visions
A closed-eye vision occurs when, obviously, the eyes are closed. The person is not asleep. He or she is fully awake but the eyelids are closed. It could come when one is in a posture of prayer or relaxation. It is in this

state of your eyes being closed to your physical surroundings that God 'opens' them to see into the supernatural. The picture could appear in varied ways: as a still, static picture; like a motion picture or a video; and sometimes, in the cause of the vision, the Lord zooms in to certain details.

Also, certain portions of the picture or image may be pronounced or very significant. It might probably not make immediate sense to the beholder, but leaves such a strong effect that it cannot be shaken off one's memory that easily. Sometimes the person understands certain portions of the image, but a sizeable part of it is confusing. When it happens like that, I believe the Lord will want the one to pray further or be very sensitive in the coming days for his instructions regarding the full vision.

PAUL'S VISION – ACTS 23:11

But the following night the Lord stood by him and said, "Be of good cheer, Paul; for as you have testified for me in Jerusalem, so you must also bear witness at Rome."

Apostle Paul had been arrested by the Jewish authorities and was in a jail in Jerusalem. His life had been threatened and no one could predict what would happen next. Whilst in the dungeon, in the middle of the night, Jesus appeared to him in a vision. This was a moving picture, because Jesus spoke and encouraged him, "Be of good cheer". Furthermore, the Lord directed him to go to Rome and bear witness of him there. By these words, Jesus was also assuring Paul that he would not be killed in Jerusalem! Hallelujah! A vision settles all questions. Truly a picture is worth more than a thousand words.

The actual import of this divine visitation was fully manifested in the events that occurred after that. More than 40 Jewish assassins devised a plan to kill Paul. But then, by divine intervention, his nephew heard of the plot and reported it to him and the commander of the jail. So, under a heavily armed guard of 200 foot soldiers and 70 horsemen, he was sent that same night to Caesarea.

Five days later, Ananias, the High Priest, arrived with some of the Jewish leaders and a distinguished orator and lawyer Tertullus, to charge Paul before Felix, the Governor of Caesarea. Listen to the charges they made against Paul:

ACTS 24:5-6,9

"For we have found this man a plague, a creator of dissension among all the Jews throughout the world and a ringleader of the sect of the Nazarenes. He even tried to profane the Temple, and we seized him and wanted to judge him according to our law." ...And the Jews also assented, maintaining that these things were so.

This was a charge that could cost him his life, but he had had a vision and therefore he could boldly defend himself in the knowledge that he was safe. The case was adjourned and Paul was placed in custody for two years. He was not perturbed, because he had had a vision. Not mere words spoken by someone who had faith, but a visitation from the Lord himself. His trials increased – from the courts of various governors to a devastating storm that lasted for 14 days in complete darkness. Then he lived through the threat of being killed by his guards, a shipwreck that left him in a strange land and being bitten by a venomous snake.

Never take the visions you receive for granted. The Lord wants you to always remember them and that is why he did not only speak to you, but showed you a picture also.

(b) Open visions

In an open vision the person's eyes are open but they are still able to see into the spirit world. You could be looking at something and then suddenly your eyes are opened beyond the natural and you begin to see spiritual things in addition to the natural.

Zechariah had an open vision

The first part of Luke Chapter 1 describes an open vision received by Zechariah the priest. Zechariah was married to Elizabeth, the cousin of Jesus' mother, Mary. They were both very old and Elizabeth who had been barren was now past menopause. As Zechariah performed his duties in the temple, an angel of the Lord appeared to him.

Zechariah was in the process of burning incense to God with his eyes wide open when the angel showed up, and he could see the angel as clearly as he saw everything else in the room.

LUKE 1:11

Then an angel of the Lord appeared to him, standing on the right side of the altar of incense.

The donkey had an open vision

Balak, the king of Moab, had sought the services of Balaam the prophet, to curse the Israelites. The Lord was furious that Balaam went with the king's messengers, so he sent an angel to stand in the road to block his way.

NUMBERS 22:22-27

Then God's anger was aroused because he went, and the angel of the LORD took his stand in the way as an adversary against him, and he was riding on his donkey and his two servants were with him. Now the donkey saw the angel of the LORD in the way with his drawn sword in his hand, and the donkey turned aside out of the way and went into the field. So Balaam struck the donkey to turn her back onto the road. Then the angel of the LORD stood in a narrow path between the vineyards, with a wall on this side and a wall on that side. And when the donkey saw the angel of the LORD, she pushed herself against the wall and crushed Balaam's foot against the wall: so he struck her again. Then the angel of the LORD went further and stood in a narrow place where there was no way to turn either to the right hand or to the left. And when the donkey saw the angel of the LORD, she lay down under Balaam; so Balaam's anger was aroused, and he struck the donkey with his staff.

After abusing the donkey so much, finally Balaam's eyes were opened and he saw beyond the natural.

There are several instances of open visions in the Scriptures, including:

(a) Samson's mother saw an angel on two occasions (Judges 13).

(b) Gideon through an open vision communicates with an angel (Judges 7).

(c) Paul after his conversion (Acts 9).

The Lord does not do such dramatic things for the pleasure of it. Everything God does, he does for a purpose. If he goes to the extent of mixing the supernatural with the natural, then there is some important information or command that the Lord is giving to you. We read in Luke Chapter 24 that soon after his resurrection, Jesus joined two disciples who were travelling to Emmaus. During this time, there were serious questions on their minds, and there was great fear among all his disciples. His exposition of the Scriptures answered their questions and allayed their fears.

These experiences are still happening today. The Lord is the same now as he was thousands of years ago, and shall be the same in the generations to come (Heb 13:8). As we become informed about these things, I pray that we shall become open to receiving information from God through his Spirit via these means.

Trances

When a person is in a trance, he gets into a state where he becomes unaware of the environment and it is characterised by the loss of voluntary movement, rigidity and a lack of sensitivity to external stimuli. The person could also be in a dazed or stunned state where it appears as though he or she is half asleep and half awake. In most cases it lasts only a few minutes; however there are times when people have been in a trance for many hours. During this time the person may feel some heaviness and see a vision and in addition receive an audible word from the Lord, or just the word without a vision or vice versa. This is another means by which the sovereign Lord communicates to his children.

In Acts 10, Peter was lodging with one Simon, a dealer in hides, in the city of Joppa. He had been fasting for some time and for some reason he decided to pray on the rooftop. He was probably feeling physically weak and that was when he fell into a trance. Then God showed him a vision of several animals that were considered by the Jews to be unclean. As Peter set eyes on these animals, the Lord commanded him, "Rise, Peter; kill and eat," but Peter refused. This happened three times.

When he came out of the trance, Peter did not know what the vision meant. But God was about to deal with years of entrenched prejudice against the Gentiles. Shortly afterwards, the Spirit of God sent Peter to the house of Cornelius, a Gentile centurion. Whilst he preached to Cornelius and his household, the Holy Spirit fell on them. In this way a lifetime belief that the Lord was only interested in Jews was dealt a devastating blow.

This experience therefore became a great foundation for him to stand up for Christian liberty, when the question of Gentiles being saved became a contentious issue – when the first general council of Christians was held in Jerusalem in Acts Chapter 15.

I fell into a trance

As a Bible school student in 1985, I went for a crusade in the Republic of Ireland. I met a young man called Michael who was suffering from schizophrenia. After the first night of the crusade, he was still in the same condition. So a pastor friend and I took him back to his home. As we were driving, Michael started to recite the whole book of Ephesians. I was so amazed I just kept saying, "Jesus let these words come to life, let these words come to life."

We drove home and I went straight to bed after we had dropped off Michael. I was just about to fall asleep when I fell into a trance. I saw a picture of a young man dressed like John the Baptist, holding the staff and clothed in camel's leather. I remember saying, "No, you are not," and he replied, "Yes, I am". I felt a presence come over me and then we had a kind of dialogue. Next, I blew wind from my mouth onto my palm, and a surge of wind and fire carried this person. Suddenly, he started changing into all kinds of shapes. Then he changed into a wild animal and I could hear him screaming and the sound gradually dying down, as though something had fallen into a deep valley. Then I came to and started thanking God. I sensed that whatever spirit was behind Michael's illness had been dealt with by God.

Early the following morning, I had a call from Michael. He said, "Pastor I am healed!" That was like music to my ears. God will use you in a trance to bring deliverance to someone and to bring a situation under control. He has confidence in you and that is why he will reveal such secrets to you. The Lord trusts you to guard these secrets and to do what he commands you to do with them.

Dreams

Everybody has had some kind of a dream before. However, they occur more frequently in some people than in others. If you do not dream, I release that ability in you to dream in Jesus' name. A dream occurs when you are asleep and your mind and all other parts of your body are at rest. It is at this time that pictures and messages float into your mind.

At this juncture, I need to make a distinction between the dreams that come as a result of the Lord speaking to you (which is what I am interested in at the moment) and those that are caused by the activity of your own soul, maybe as a result of eating heavily before sleeping.

Dreams are one of the ways by which the Lord communicates with us. There are several examples of God using dreams to communicate to his people throughout the Bible.

Direction through dreams

In Genesis 40, Pharaoh's chief butler and chief baker both had dreams during their incarceration. Upon narrating their dreams to Joseph, he tells them the interpretations, which are confirmed when, in three days, the butler is released and restored to his position but the baker is executed.

In the New Testament, we read that Joseph, the 'father' of Jesus, had been informed by his fiancée that she was expecting a child conceived by the Holy Ghost. Knowing that she was supposed to have been a virgin, and as a righteous man, he resolved to break up the engagement. But as he thought about this he fell asleep and the Bible says,

MATTHEW 1:20

...Behold, an angel of the Lord appeared to him in a dream, saying, "Joseph, son of David, do not be afraid. Take to you Mary your wife, for that which is conceived in her is of the Holy Spirit."

Through the dream the Lord settled the confusion that had arisen in Joseph and imminent disgrace that would have come to Mary if Joseph had gone ahead with his decision to break off the engagement.

After this incident, there were three more instances recorded in Matthew chapter two, where Joseph is instructed through dreams concerning the baby Jesus. In Matthew 2:13, the Lord commanded Joseph in a dream to flee to Egypt with Mary and the baby because King Herod had planned to kill the child. When Herod died, an angel again appeared to Joseph in Egypt and reported it to him and instructed him to go back to Israel. Finally in another dream, he was warned to go to Galilee.

God is determined to direct us concerning things that are in the future, so let us be open to his instructions that come through dreams. When you wake up out of a dream, you may not remember the whole dream but there are certain parts that you remember vividly. Do not disregard them, note them down and, as events unfold, you will receive clarity in its meaning.

Your response to visions, trances and dreams is very important. The significance you give to these means by which God speaks to you will enable you to take possession of whatever message God will give to you through the 'eye gate'.

I want you to take note of these facts about the various manifestations I have discussed with you so far.

In a trance, closed-eye vision or an open vision, there could be dialogue. You may not need to open your mouth to have dialogue with the Lord, but during the experience you will be aware of discourse.

1. All these manifestations are available for the children of God to experience in this age.

2. As you take time to learn about them, it will create a desire in you that will cause the Lord to minister to you through these means.

3. Experiences of this nature could occur anywhere at all – at home, in church, or even whilst resting at a park – so be ready.

The sense of hearing – the 'ear gate'

The ears are for hearing. Through this medium, you hear a word from the Lord, which nobody else hears but you alone.

I shall now take you through a teaching on the various ways in which we can hear the voice of God.

The audible voice

As the boy Samuel was sleeping by the Ark of the Covenant in the temple in Shiloh, he heard somebody call out his name, "Samuel, Samuel". He thought that Eli, the priest, was the man calling him, because the sound was coming from that direction. So he ran up to the elderly Eli who was also sleeping and asked him, "Sir, did you call?" Eli asked him to go back to sleep, because he had not called him. This happened two more times until, after the third call, the experienced priest told Samuel that it was the Lord that was calling him and then taught him how to respond (1 Samuel 3:1-10).

It is interesting that Eli, the priest, did not hear anything during all the time that the Lord was speaking to Samuel. Even though the Lord was speaking in an audible voice, his message was to Samuel's spiritual ear, hence no one else could hear.

Once I was in my room when I heard my name, "Sam" and I replied, "Who is it?" Right then I knew it was the Lord trying to speak with me, so I stayed silent to hear him. The Lord did not continue however, so I spent some time praying about it and I believe he took care of whatever it was.

Saul heard a voice

Saul (who later became Paul) was on his way to Damascus with a group of soldiers. Along the way a bright light, much brighter than the Middle East noon, brought him to his knees. Then a voice said, "Saul, Saul, why are you persecuting me?" Saul answered, "Who are you Lord?" The Lord then spoke extensively to Saul; although his companions heard the sound of a voice, they could not hear the words that were spoken (Acts 9:1-7).

I heard an audible voice

Many years ago I had applied for British citizenship and for about nine months I had been waiting for the immigration office to grant my request. One day, as we were at a prayer meeting, the word of the Lord came to me, "Knew ye not whence this was done?" You can see by the language he used that God has a good sense of humour.

If he had spoken in everyday English I may probably have not taken it very seriously, but when I sensed him speaking in ancient English, I instantly knew that the Lord had answered. This was 25th April 1983. Three days later a postman brought a parcel and there, inside the envelope, was the passport I had been waiting for. When I looked at the 'Date of Issue', I saw to my amazement, 25th April 1983, the day the Lord's word came to me.

Why will the Almighty God speak to a simple man like me? I believe that it is because he loves me. He loves you in the same way and that is the reason why he will communicate with you. He loves you. Only believe. Remember that only the supernatural ear can hear the voice of the supernatural God.

Impression

Apart from the audible voice of God, there may also be a deep impression. Sometimes an intuitional power or certain knowledge of something comes over you and you know that something has been said to you. This is the difference between "And God said to..." and "The word of the Lord came to..." (1King 18:1).

When the word of the Lord comes to you, it bears a strong impression on one subject or another. This is one way through which the Lord speaks to us. There are instances also when it comes without much heralding and clarity.

Sometimes the Spirit of God may refer you to a Scripture. As you read the Scripture, some particular words will overwhelm you and a certain revelation comes to you. That is God speaking to you. Prayer will cease to be boring when the Lord is dealing with you in all these ways.

The sense of touch – the 'feeling gate'

There is a popular song about not being moved by our feelings that I agree with very much. This is how the song goes:

Amen Amen
Amen Amen Amen
I am not moved by what I feel, Hallelujah!
I am not moved by what I feel, Hallelujah!

We cannot depend on how we feel because how we feel at any moment can easily be determined by the circumstances we face. Therefore it is necessary for us, as Christians, to rather focus on what the Lord says about our situation than how we feel about it. But, at the risk of sounding as though I am contradicting myself, I must say that the Lord sometimes communicates with us through the way we feel.

Corresponding pain

As a preacher, there are instances when I will feel a sharp pain on a certain part of my body. Due to my long association with the Holy Spirit and the depth of the relationship, right away I recognise this as God's healing power desiring to reach somebody in the congregation with an ailment in that part of the body. Then I call out, "There is someone here with a pain in your side, the Lord is healing you right now." And true to his prompting, the person comes to confirm it. That is not to say that that is the only way through which the Lord talks to the man of God to speak the word of healing.

Sometimes, in a prayer meeting, you can suddenly feel a severe backache. If you are not sensitive, you might just assume that it is a passing bout of tiredness. But it may be that the Lord had chosen you to stand in prayer on somebody's behalf. As you exercise your authority and rebuke the pain or whatever it may be, in the name of Jesus you will realise that that pain just lifts – almost in the same way as it came. In time you will come to hear how someone was delivered from something similar at about the same time as you felt it. When it so happens, do not go about bragging about it, but thank God for using you in this way. If, on the other hand, you do not receive any confirmation, still go ahead and give thanks to God.

Corresponding situation

This particular situation is similar to the corresponding pain, but in this case, you do not feel any pain but some overpowering feeling, such as fear. When you search your heart for what could be the reason, you find no good reason why you should feel that way. I believe that at that moment, the Lord is allowing you to share in another person's fear – so that you could stand in on their behalf to intercede.

When this comes to you, do not doubt, just exercise faith and command that thing to go. Sometimes after you pray the situation persists. Tell your pastor, house group or fellow believers to help you deal with it.

Take note that not all attacks of fear you receive are the promptings of God for you to pray for somebody. It may also be an attack of the devil on your courage. Do not allow it to overwhelm you and make you do things outside the Word of God. Some time ago, prior to elections in South Africa, a gentleman stood up in a large church and prophesied: "There is a great fear coming home, fear, fear, it's so fearful that I (God) myself I'm afraid." Thankfully the pastor asked the congregation to ignore the prophecy. Obviously the gentleman was so scared that he felt even God must have been going through the same fears.

The sense of smell – the 'nose gate'

Everything on earth bears a particular smell. Many times the smell of an object, rather than its look or sound is what is used to determine what it is. The same phenomenon applies in the spiritual realm. As you become more experienced in spiritual things, you will find out that demons have a certain odour, and any time you smell it in any place or on someone, you will immediately know that a demon is present.

Once we wanted to hire a hall in London for a church service. The landlord who was a Christian took me into the room and this is what he said, "This place smells like... this place is like..." He would not say what. But when we came out he told me that he sensed demonic presence at the place. Apparently, the place was haunted. After we had prayed, we noticed the difference. God can use your nose to detect demonic presence.

The sense of taste – the 'mouth gate'

2 KINGS 4:39-41

...One went out into the field to gather herbs, and found a wild vine, and gathered from it a lapful of wild gourds, and came and sliced them into the pot of stew, although they did not know what they were. Then they served it to the men to eat. Now it happened, as they were eating the stew, that they cried out and said, "Man of God, there is death in the pot!" and they could not eat it. So he said, "Then bring some flour." He put it into the pot

and said, "Serve it to the people that they may eat."
And there was nothing harmful in the pot.

This phenomenon does not often happen, but God uses it anyhow when he needs to. As was the case of the men with Elijah, you may be offered food, which may be very appetising and mouth watering. But as soon as you taste it, you are jolted by its awful taste. This may be the strongest message the Lord will give you to stop you from eating that which will harm you. Take the cue and do not allow your hunger to overpower you.

CAUTION

Any experienced Christian will tell you that they have seen so many of God's gifts mishandled by believers who claimed to be led by the Holy Spirit. It is important that we do not deviate or take everything to the extreme and thereby be led by our own human desires and abilities. This is what causes people to be put off by such beautiful manifestations of the blessed Holy Spirit. The best way to operate them is in love and humility. God desires to communicate with us more than we even do. Therefore, let us move along with the Lord as we do all things in decency and order.

Here are a few simple things you can do to encourage the growth of these gifts in you. Have a pen, paper and a lamp by your bedside. This will enable you to record any dream that the Lord gives to you, so that you do not have to toil to recollect it.

Remember that pride neutralises godly power. Sadly, when some prayerful people begin to experience these things, they become so proud and boastful. Obviously, this is not God's purpose at all in giving you these manifestations. In no time you will find out that these things stop occurring in your life.

I suggest that when the Lord reveals something to you concerning another person do not tell them directly. Pray and speak to your pastor about it first. If you saw their right leg amputated, what good will it do to tell them? Often we create panic, when the Lord has only revealed to redeem. God is not the author of confusion.

The best gift is that which is exercised at the proper time and under the authority of the leadership that God has given over you. Be open and make yourself available for God to use you in his kingdom. When you start operating in these areas, there may be times when you will doubt and not be sure, but keep at it. Do not be afraid of the devil, because whatever he says will always be against Scripture and will also create confusion.

You are an important member of the army of God. God is arming you for battle, so that with the divine information he gives, you will know when and how to deploy the power that is available to you. It is the Lord's desire that you will not throw aimless punches that do not land and that, rather, you will use limited effort to achieve much.

CHAPTER SIX

Harmony in Prayer

One of the most important tools of prayer is the mind. The mind is crucial in prayer because it is also that which can easily be distracted, nullifying the effect of the energy of several hours spent before the Lord. Every Christian who prays can testify of the many battles we have had to wage on the mind to bring it into subjection and keep it from wandering. In this chapter, I will explain the make-up of the mind so that you will better appreciate its role in prayer.

MATTHEW 22:37-38

Jesus said to him, "You shall love the Lord your God with all your heart, with all your soul, and with all your mind. This is the first and great commandment.

Jesus taught that there are three ingredients that we need to bring to the Lord when we come into prayer – the heart, soul and mind. Therefore, how should we pray? We must bring our heart, our soul and our mind into agreement for effective prayer to be done.

Aligning the heart, which is also known as the spirit (and please note that I am talking about the spirit of man that indwells man and not the Holy Spirit), with the mind calls for total agreement within one's being. The human being is a spirit but he has a soul and he dwells in a body. And it is necessary to bring the mind, which is part of the soul, into agreement with the spirit.

The unconscious, subconscious and conscious

The mind is a culmination of three components: the unconscious, the subconscious and the conscious. The unconscious forms the part of the mind containing instincts, impulses, images and ideas that are not available for direct examination. The unconscious mind contains all kinds of information stored over the years, which is not readily accessible, and the subconscious is the part of the mind outside or only partly within one's conscious awareness.

From time to time information in these parts of the mind filters into the conscious, creating all kinds of confusion. Sometimes they come in as dreams and tend to dominate the conscious. As the body is world-conscious, the spirit of man is God-conscious. The soul, which is the embodiment of the mind, will, and emotion, is self-conscious.

The Spirit of Christ dwells in the spirit of man when he becomes born-again. The new birth in Christ means the spirit of man is connected back to its original source of spiritual life – God. The spirit then becomes a perfect entity, which responds directly to the Word of God.

The influences of the mind

The mind comes under many influences. It is not directly related to God, like the spirit of man, hence the mind has to be tuned to that part of man which after regeneration has become a perfect entity, namely the born again spirit of a man. This opens the possibility for the mind to be aligned to the human spirit. So, as you read the Word of God, it can now make sense to you. Aligning the mind with the spirit involves bringing the mind into agreement with the Spirit and the Word of God.

The extent to which the mind feeds on the Word of God controls the degree of alignment the spirit has with the mind. The entrance of the Word gives light (Ps 119:130). The truth of the Word releases the light that invades the darkness in the unconscious, subconscious and the conscious mind, helping it to align with the spirit.

When we receive the truth of the Word of God into our spirit, our mind becomes full of light. Then we can say, "Your word is a light for my path" (Ps 119:105). This results in harmony and agreement within a person's being. There is tranquillity and peace. When Paul advises us to put on the helmet of salvation (Eph 6:17), he is asking us to protect our mind from all kinds of misinformation and ridding it also of all undesirable pieces of information acquired throughout one's life.

When this agreement is achieved, power is released, so that struggles to focus in prayer or just saying repetitive prayers are conquered. Intimacy with the Lord Jesus develops out of this harmony. The greater the harmony, the closer we are with Jesus.

The whole counsel of God takes a seat inside man's spirit when we believe the good news and receive Jesus in our hearts. The very breath of God was put inside us and this connected us to the throne of the universe. As a result of that, man became limitless with what we could do with prayer. Our prayer now travels faster than the speed of light. We can touch anywhere on the globe with our prayer. What a tremendous source of power and influence!

JAMES 5:16

The effective, fervent prayer of a righteous man avails much.

The Christian thus becomes the most powerful being on earth. The full abilities of the Word of God are placed at his disposal and he becomes a major threat to the devil. Such a prayer can only come out of a being where harmony prevails and agreement between mind and spirit is at its peak.

The noise level

Another important reason for mind and spirit to be in harmony is because of what I call the 'noise level'. This is the amount of interference in your thought patterns as you focus to pray. Noise interrupts our concentration and lessens the power in our prayer. When the noise level in the mind is reduced, that is when the mind is disciplined and then we will be able to bring the mind and spirit into harmony.

The 'noise' is not limited to the sense of hearing only but pervades all the five senses – by which man relates to this physical world. When you decide to pray, mundane things in life such as shopping, a reply to a letter, and cooking, seem to take on a life of their own and demand your attention.

The television seems to cry out to you, "Please watch me," unnecessary phone calls choose that moment to come in, food in the refrigerator beckons you to have a bite, and your bed will not keep quiet either, screaming at you, "Hey! Why don't you take a quick nap for a few minutes". All these affect your focus on prayer; hence personal self-discipline is required at all times to deal with the noise level.

The noise of accusation

Sometimes, as you get ready to pray, some weird, wild thoughts attack your thoughts. Thoughts of past failures and reasons why God will not hear your prayer, because of past sins weighing on your mind. The devil, also known as the 'Accuser of the Brethren', has often resorted to this trick of making us feel unworthy. The purpose of this noise is to cause the prayer session to be aborted.

He knows us in advance

ROMANS 8:29, 30, 33, 34

For whom he foreknew, he also predestined to be conformed to the image of his Son, that he might be the firstborn among many brethren. Moreover, whom he predestined, these he also called, whom he called, these he also justified: and whom he justified, these he also glorified. Who shall bring a charge against God's elect? It is God who justifies. Who is he who condemns? It is Christ who died, and furthermore is also risen, who is even at the right hand of God, who also makes intercession for us.

Jesus had you in mind when he hung on the cross at Calvary. When there are questions about your unworthiness, remember that according to the Scripture above, he knew everything about you, and still went ahead to sacrifice his life for you. Jesus has already paid your debt. There is only one person who condemns you and that is the devil. So when he speaks, shout back and make him aware that you know who you are in Christ and therefore you cannot be condemned!

The devil is the father and originator of lies (John 8:44). His lies will cripple your faith and cause you to cast doubts on what the Word of God says. When you take in his lies, it will release numbness into your faith, which makes you unable to receive or give out power. That is the crippling nature of his attack. His intention is to get you to doubt the truth of the Word of God. One cannot believe the Word of God and the lies of the devil at the same time.

The battle plan of Satan

As believers, we should be familiar with the strategies and the battle plan of Satan. They should not take us by surprise because we are in a war. As a former officer in the army, I will now say a bit about one of the principles of war.

In the army there are different phases of war. In each phase, commanders of various levels are encouraged to seize the initiative at all times. To do this, a commander has got to adhere to certain principles pertaining to that phase of war. Principles are not rigid laws or regulations and their non-adherence does not attract any punishment as such but can be very costly. In the phase of attack on the enemy, all commanders at any given level, know that once the attack has commenced, its 'momentum' must be maintained. This calls for any supporting elements to keep up with the pace of the attack. Air strikes, naval gun support and artillery fire must be carefully synchronised with the advancing foot soldiers who close in on the enemy and destroy him.

Prayer can be likened to this phase of war. You cannot go on a prayer holiday or allow it to become an ineffective ritual or a routine. You must strive to maintain the momentum. In order to do that you have to fill your mind with the Word of God and God's heartbeat – winning the lost into the kingdom of God. Satan hates to lose territory. His territory is the hearts of men and women, boys and girls.

When an army is on the advance, they do so to make contact with the enemy. Their focus is to get to the main stronghold of the enemy's forces. However, as the enemy retreats, they leave pockets of resistance along the line of advance of the invading army. It is up to the invading army to see these resistances as distractions aimed at slowing down its advance. The commanders ensure that the ferocity of the attack is maintained and that concentration is focused on the main target.

The praying Christian will also suffer attacks by various pockets of resistance, which come as mental, emotional and physical attacks. Things that will cause one's spirit to be unsettled, hence it becomes difficult to focus on Jesus and have proper direction and guidance from the Holy Spirit.

Ministries that stir up faith in people come under different attacks over and over again. But this is a sign that they are making advances against the devil. At such times, it is important to stay focused, because God is faithful, and by the Holy Spirit we shall have victory and be promoted.

CHAPTER SEVEN

National Prayer Brings... Revival Time!

The National Prayer Summit

The Lord laid on my heart to organise a National Prayer Summit in London. This was started in March of 1998, and is now held twice yearly in March and September. Several hundreds of believers around the country gathered to corporately intercede for the UK. The needs of other countries are also covered during the summit.

One Sunday morning in May 2000, the Lord spoke to my heart, "Europe has turned her back on me and now trusting only in technology. If she would not repent, I will cause air pollution, water pollution and spread of skin diseases to affect the nations of Europe." I was very much afraid but the thought that came to my spirit was that the National Prayer Summit could intercede for Europe and at the same time make Europe aware of this damning prophecy. The Lord reveals to redeem but folks have got to intercede by corporate repentance to meet the just demands of a just God. We picked this issue up very seriously at our 'All-day Wednesday' Prayer Meeting at our Church Headquarters in Camberwell whilst informing other Christian leaders of the prophecy.

The outbreak of Foot and Mouth Disease coincided with our September 2000 National Prayer Summit. Foot and Mouth Disease is an acute viral disease of cattle, pigs, sheep and goats. The spread of the disease in England was getting very serious at this time. Europe was becoming nervous; travellers from the United Kingdom into Europe were subjected to all kinds of scrutiny at their ports of entry. We were motivated to pray more and recruit others into it. Wherever I spoke outside of my platform, I talked about the prophecy the Lord had given me.

We now can thank and praise the Lord that Foot and Mouth Disease is over. Corporate intercession works!

Revival is a word that has gained some popularity in recent times. Whenever there is a need for revival, it means that something is dying or is dead. God's desire for Christians is that we will always be like salt wherever we are, giving life and preserving the tenets of Christianity in all situations. Many places need the life of God, without which, many will be lost to hell forever. One of the pervading truths in the Scriptures is that God is not happy when sinners die in their sins and that it is his will that all should come to salvation.

Sin is a reproach to any nation. It attracts the judgment of God and because God is a just God, when sin abounds judgment also abounds. When people realise their sinfulness and cry out to God, his mercy is released. The sin is forgiven, remembered no more, and thereby the deserved punishment is averted.

God is a just God and his demands are just. His call for us to confess our sins and ask for the blood of Jesus to intercede for us is a just demand. We are now ready for the revival. Revival will come because the Lord has promised it and he is faithful to his word.

God is going to revive according to his justice.

PSALM 119:149

...O Lord, revive me according to your justice.

Once we get convinced that we need a revival in our church or nation, we must be confident to ask God for that revival because God will give us the revival for the sake of his word. Then we can pray like the psalmist: "...revive me according to your word" (Psalm 119:154), and expect an answer.

God is such a loving and caring God and, because of that, he will release revival for his people.

PSALM 119:159

...Revive me, O Lord, according to your loving kindness.

We do not want to face the judgment of God and that is why we need revival. When we cry out to God his mercy is released and it drives judgment away. Revival comes in answer to humble prayer. With the first signs of revival, the Holy Spirit's presence, power and glory are experienced and loved by his people. This causes them to trust God more, desire more revival and therefore live holier lives and pray more effectually and fervently. The increased effectual prayer brings down the rain of God's mercy, which releases more prayer and the cycle continues (Ps 37:4).

Unfortunately, the attitude of some Christians today is as though God is powerless to do anything, let alone bring a revival. Let us think the way God thinks and believe that he desires to give us revival. This is the time to cry out, "Lord revive us according to your loving kindness. Lord revive us according to your word. Lord revive us according to your justice." And it shall happen.

Praying together for the revival

JEREMIAH 33:3

Call to me, and I will answer you...

Whenever we come together to pray, the Lord hears and he answers. In Acts chapter twelve, James the brother of John had been killed and Peter was in jail awaiting execution. In order to ensure that Peter did not escape, he was chained to two soldiers and surrounded by others. It was in this time of extreme persecution that the church gathered together in the house of Mary, the mother of John Mark, to pray. The church prayed out of desperation. "God must act! God must intervene," they seemed to be saying.

At the same time as they prayed, God dispatched an angel from heaven to go and release Peter from jail. The angels are waiting in heaven to be dispatched to earth to rescue us from any prison we may find ourselves in. As we gather to pray, the Lord releases angels to free us from every bondage in our marriages, every bondage of drugs, homosexuality, adultery and all the degradation that has entered the Church.

Did you know that in 1973 one woman caused an amendment to the American Constitution? A 14-year-old girl had been raped and she became pregnant. This woman fought for the girl to be allowed to abort the child, to which the Supreme Court agreed. As a result of this, abortion became legalised and in the past 15 years, there have been more than 35 million abortions in America alone.

By God's grace, this woman has become a born again Christian. At a national prayer summit, she confessed that whenever she sleeps, she sees the children's play grounds all over America completely empty, without any children in them. She used that platform to confess the awesome burden on her soul and to receive emotional and mental healing. But the point here is that we Christians have access to the greatest power in the universe. Through prayer we can draw on that power to change the constitutions of nations. God is more powerful than the Supreme Court of the most powerful nation in the world. Are we prepared to pay the price in patient, persistent, believing prayer?

The conditions for a revival

There are two Scriptures that relate to sin and the situation. Proverb 14:34 states "Righteousness exalts a nation, but sin is a reproach to any people." The other Scripture that hits sin at the very core when we pray for our nations is this passage in the Old Testament:

2 CHRONICLES 7:14

If my people, who are called by my name will humble themselves, and pray and seek my face, and turn from their wicked ways, then I will hear from heaven, and will forgive their sin and heal their land.

The conditional word 'if' sets the tone of this Scripture. The Lord is saying that even though we are his people, there are certain requirements we must fulfil for him to give us his attention. We must become humble. In practical terms humility means that we must stop depending on ourselves; redirect our trust entirely on God and not lean on our own understanding (Prov 3:5).

The Lord promises that, "then I will hear from heaven and will forgive their sin and heal their land." This is his heart-warming assurance that once the conditions are met, he will hear from heaven and forgive our sin. God's kindness is far beyond what we can comprehend, but he is constrained by his principles. Therefore his helping hand is only set in motion if we satisfy the requirements he has set in his Word. In much the same way that he does not want us to compromise on our Christian character, God also cannot compromise on his holiness and justice. He cannot ignore the sin in our lives and cannot brush it aside to bless. No. In order for him to come to our assistance, he demands that we seek forgiveness and cleansing for the sin first, before the lines of communication and provision will be opened.

Jesus trusted us enough to give us the responsibility to make disciples of every tribe, race and nation. He has given us the authority to turn them into members of the family of God. He will surely hear us when we pray for our nation. Petition him night and day and he will surely respond to your call for a revival.

The joy of revival

In Acts 8, Philip went to the city of Samaria and preached about Jesus there. He proclaimed the good news about Jesus dying to pay the penalty for sin so we can receive forgiveness for our sins. He emphasised the fact that Jesus was raised up on the third day after his death and is alive for ever more. His proclamation was confirmed with signs and wonders. Demons were cast out of people, the lame walked, the blind saw, the hopeless had something to look forward to, the dark clouds that had hung over the city of Samaria for a very long time were lifted – there was a revival.

ACTS 8:8

And there was great joy in that city.

The praise of God filled homes, and many had testimonies of healing and deliverance. Discipline returned to individual lives; thieves stopped stealing and became honest; liars spoke the truth; broken marriages were restored; runaway children returned home and people's lives were transformed. What a revival!

Often we rely on our condition when we pray rather than focusing on our position in Christ. By the atoning work of Jesus on the cross, access was created for all to reconnect to God. Jesus became the bridge for us to get to God. His death brought about the reconciliation between man and God. Sons of men can now become sons of God. The guilt of sin was permanently removed and anybody who calls on the name of the Lord can be saved. Our position now is that of sonship.

Watching for our land

To watch is to be 'awake' and to be alert and on the look out (Luke 21:36; 1 Cor 16:13; Eph 6:18; 1 Peter 5:8).

ISAIAH 62:6-7

I have set watchmen on your walls, O Jerusalem; they shall never hold their peace day or night. You who make mention of the Lord, do not keep silent. And give him no rest, till he establishes, and till he makes Jerusalem a praise in the earth.

God has "set" us to be watchmen. As believers, we have been entrusted with the authority and responsibility to be watchmen over nations and cities. As watch-men, we are expected to be on the look-out for any danger from without and from within that threatens our towns, our cities and nations. We have been called to take care of what goes on inside the land as well as outside. Our concentration must be on making sure that all goes well within and we have a duty to protect our territory from being overrun by the forces outside or any that may have slipped in. We cannot let our guard down; God is counting on us.

God's plan is that his house will become a praise on the earth. Anytime the name of Jerusalem is mentioned peace, healing and joy must be released. God has hand-picked you for that reason. The fact that the Lord hand-picked you means that your role is of great value to him.

The Lord himself has positioned you strategically at the observation and listening posts. The work is observation by day and listening by night, thereby providing an all-round 24-hour watch. This requires watchmen with good eyesight and ears that are opened at all times.

The Lord has placed his prayer mantle on us with a specific responsibility, to ensure that Jerusalem in Israel is established and, secondly, that our own Jerusalem (capital cities representing our nations) shall also be established. Jeremiah 29:7 commands us to seek the peace and prosperity of the city. Pray to the Lord for it because if it prospers you too will prosper. We are to pray for the establishment of the kingdom of God – the rule, domin-ion and reign of God as King, in the hearts of men.

The Lord desires to show us the way. We can never get direction from our own efforts. There is no way we can get the sinners to come in and the backsliders to be restored in our own strength. Any time there has been a bumper harvest of souls, it has come through believers who saw the need and gathered to pray for a revival. We need a revival today. You can begin as a man or woman of prayer and bring others into that vision. And as you communicate with God, you will hear from him and you would have divine direction for a revival.

Corporate and Group Prayer (or the Church at Prayer)

PROVERBS 29:18

Where there is no revelation, the people cast off restraint; but happy is he who keeps the law.

The Church of Jesus Christ must have a vision. Our mission must be to bring Jesus into the community. We must permeate whatever goes on in our communities with the message and character of Jesus.

For the church to be relevant to the community and nation in which it is located, it must be a praying church in the knowledge that it can never be defeated (Matt 16:18). "Where two or three are gathered together in my name, I am in their midst"(Matt 18:20). Such a praying church must have a leadership that follows certain principles.

Principle 1: Identification

There are different problems that prevail in different communities. If you take a good look at your community you will notice certain peculiarities that carry on from generation to generation. It is important to come together as a church to trace the problem and pray about it. The recurring problems have a main cause which if not tackled will continue to manifest.

A story is told of a city in Canada where every treasurer that was appointed misappropriated money. It did not matter how high the integrity of that person was, in no time after his appointment he embezzled money. After many years of this cycle of embezzlement, some believers started to pray about it. Then they made an amazing discovery. The first person who has been appointed treasurer had stolen money and this had attracted a spirit of misappropriation that affected anyone who was appointed to that office.

How did they deal with that issue? They went before God and confessed on behalf of the city. Afterwards, they asked for his forgiveness and it worked. Sin gives the devil a legal right to interfere. If you sin and do not confess to God and ask for forgiveness, you just open the door to the enemy. The devil is like a salesman; if you open your door to him, he immediately places his foot inside, looks you in the eyes and forces his way in. Unconfessed sin gives him access to your life.

When he enters he does not sit down or even accept tea or coffee. He is trained to sell first before allowing any pleasures. He perceives anything other than selling his products as a distraction. No prayer warrior or other believer should delay whenever he goes wrong. Come back to God quickly, confess the sin, ask for forgiveness and keep the devil out. Give the devil no place.

Principle 2: Spiritual mapping

To find the spiritual root causes of traits and behavioural patterns, or even policies of leaders, in a community or nation is called 'spiritual mapping'. So when a group of believers come together to intercede for a family, tribe, community, nation, etc, they need to seek God's face for direction regarding demonic stronghold. They will have to go into a period of fasting and prayer as the Lord directs them, not individually but corporately, with that community in mind. This is not the same as having conferences, crusades, and seminars about the particular community. These sessions do not influence governments who are the decision makers. Even though it is God who allows each government to come into power, some of their decisions and policies are directed from hell and that is why we need to tackle them by prayer. Only prayer influences government.

In England, if you want accommodation from the Local Council, you could be on the waiting list for many years. The rent for these flats is subsidised so the Councils have requests from far more people than they can accommodate.

Therefore, the Councils came up with a policy that gave priority to pregnant women or women with children. This caused teenage girls to throw all caution to the wind, and sleep with any man, so they would become pregnant. Not only would they get accommodation but, in addition, they would receive a weekly allowance from the state for the upkeep of each child. So the more children one has, the more money one gets and the larger and nicer the house you are given. Guess what, there are now huge numbers of children without fathers; this generates increasing waywardness among children and eventually a rising crime rate.

We are now reaping the results of a policy that was thought to be a good idea in the beginning but has been proved over time to be daft. It is very obvious that this was not a God-driven policy. Hence, when believers come together in corporate prayer, through spiritual mapping we find out the root cause of such issues and are able to deal with them at the source.

When we pray for our community through this means we are able to target the particular problems at stake and will not pray blindly. The wellbeing of our community is so important because our peace as individuals depends on it (1 Timothy 2:2). We can change the spirit ruling our locality, and that responsibility lies with all believers coming together in unity to pray.

The Calli experience
Calli, a city in Colombia, was plagued with murder and drugs. This persisted for many years and the security forces had no answer. A preacher tried getting all Christians together to pray, but they could not be united. Then the Holy Spirit told the preacher that God was

going to heal the land but at a great cost to the pastor. One day as he went to a meeting, he was assassinated. This brought together all the Christian leaders in that city to start praying. Denominational barriers came down and huge numbers of people started coming to Christ. Everybody got involved to pray.

The drug cartels were losing their influence on the people and their leaders were being arrested, and it was a major news item the first day there was no murder in the city. All the newspapers carried it as their front-page news. Now Calli has become a peaceful city without any resemblance to its dreadful past. The responsibility for directing the affairs of your nation rests on you.

Principle 3: Confess publicly

When leaders come together to pray after spiritual mapping, it is absolutely essential that those praying lift up the sins of the community (or home) before the Lord. This means to confess the sins of the land by name and ask for God's forgiveness. The leader must identify with those sins. We have a right to get out of it, because the Lord has promised that when we confess our sins, we will be forgiven.

This procedure of receiving deliverance from demonic influences does not only apply to communities and cities, but can be used for the deliverance of households. After moving into a new house, you may encounter certain distressing patterns or nightmares. What do you do?

You must come together as a family and confess the sins that have been committed over the years in that house. As you do this, any 'legal' base that gave the devil power to operate in that house will be broken.

1 JOHN 4:4

You are of God, little children, and have overcome them, because he who is in you is greater than he who is in the world.

The omnipotent blessed Holy Spirit dwells inside you and gives you the authority to ask for any evil oppressive power operating within and over your household to be broken. Many Christians behave like a person holding a big club who, when confronted by a small snake, becomes so petrified that he takes to his heels shouting, "Snake! Snake!" Instead of turning round and striking it on the head, they keep running and shouting. You are a Christian. You have power through the Holy Spirit who indwells you. Strike at the devil. Pray and be free!

Sometimes you find couples reduced to the state of constant bickering and fighting. Whatever problem exists never seems to be resolved. Take a break from the fighting and spend some time to pray for your marriage. It is time for a revolution!

There are some problems that run through families and go on from generation to generation. As you take time to seek the face of God about your situation, he will cause you to see the similarities that run through your family and how like your father or mother and the generations before him or her, you seem to be saddled with the same kind of wife or husband, respectively. The power is in your hands; the answer to the deliverance of your marriage is in the name of Jesus.

Principle 4: Taking authority

The devil is an illegal immigrant. An illegal immigrant is a person who enters any country without a visa or the proper travelling documents. Such a person is arrested by the authorities and summarily deported. From the day Jesus came into your life, Satan was rendered an illegal settler. Kick him out!

The devil uses certain strategically placed people within churches to hold back the work the Lord wants to do. Let us come together to pray. Prayer is the key and prayer will smoke out all evil.

When the deliverance comes do not stop praying, sustain the deliverance by continuous prayer. It is extremely important that you maintain the newness that the Lord gives you for yourself, your home or your community.

JESUS CAUTIONS – MATTHEW 12:43-45

"When an unclean spirit goes out of a man, he goes through dry places, seeking rest, and finds none. Then he says, "I will return to my house from which I came." And when he comes, he finds it empty, swept and put in order. Then he goes and takes with him seven other spirits more wicked than himself, and they enter and dwell there and the last state of that man is worse than the first. So shall it also be with this wicked generation."

In Acts 12:1-18, we read of the Church at prayer. God had to respond to those audacious prayers and sent an angel to release Peter from prison. I believe the Church was also at prayer when we read that God sent an angel to release John and Peter from jail (Acts 5:17-26).

CHAPTER NINE

The Intercessor

JAMES 5:16, 17

Therefore confess your sins to each other and pray for each other so that you may be healed. The prayer of a righteous man is powerful and effective. Elijah was a man just like us. He prayed earnestly that it would not rain on the land for three-and-a-half years.

ISAIAH 53:12

Therefore I will divide him a portion with the great, and he shall divide the spoil with the strong, because he poured out his soul unto death, and he was numbered with the transgressors, and he bore the sin of many, and made intercession for the transgressors.

Who are you in him? The devil is so afraid of you that he will suggest to you that you cannot be an intercessor. He makes you think that this is a special office for the pastor and a few old-time Christians who do no wrong. So I ask you now, who saved you? Who called you and who will equip you? It is he whose duty it is equip you. He saw something worthy in you that he could use and that is why he called you!

JAMES 15:16

You did not choose me, but I choose you "to go and bear fruit" – fruit that will last. Then the Father will give you whatever you ask in my name.

The good news is that Jesus believes in you. He who is greater than you believes in you. You ought to know this so that when you stand praying, you pray like someone who has been hand-picked and chosen by the most powerful Person, who created all things. As you believe that God believes in you, you must release your faith and believe that divine power is going to flow out of your lips.

I believe that I carry the power of God in me. I assure you that I am not saying this because I am a senior pastor, but because I know Jesus believes in me. I depend on God's Word and so I must believe it too. In England a lot of people ask, "Why do you have to pray for long hours? We are not hungry, people have jobs and everything is OK." Fortunately, there are a lot of people like me who do not see things in this way. When I go through various communities, I feel the degradation, the incest, promiscuity, drunkenness, murder, adultery and wickedness that plague us. I know that these things grieve the Lord so much and so they grieve me also. I believe that it is for this cause that the Lord has set us up in the place we are, so that we can hold in check the work of the devil in the lives of our people. It is the intercessor's duty to have the heart of God for the community.

We were driving in a neighbourhood when a pastor friend told me that the area was full of crime. The radio was on and just then we heard that somebody had been shot twice in the head, right in that neighbourhood. Can you imagine how the Lord feels about this? He desires that you will be an intercessor and cry out to him concerning yourself, your home, your church, your community and your nation.

When you pray, God lifts you up towards him. Every time you intercede he draws you a little higher, closer to where he is and you will see things more in the way he sees them. The evil around you must push you to a place of desperation. You see, when you are in a state of desperation you will not let sleep overtake you. You will want to stand there and pray, and pray and pray your heart out.

Qualifications of the intercessor

It is important to remember that all Christians are called to be intercessors.

Here are a number of things the intercessor must do:

- The intercessor must pray in other tongues. From the day you give your life to Christ, God puts the ability to pray in other tongues in you. I shall discuss this in more detail in Chapter 10. However you must exercise faith, relying on God to reveal that truth to you. Once the Holy Spirit enlightens you and you see the truth of the promise (Mark 16:17; Acts 2:4; Acts 10:46) and you exercise your faith, you can speak in tongues.

- Humility is another cardinal requirement for every intercessor. As you become an intercessor, times will come when the Lord will reveal certain truths about somebody or a community to you, for you to pray about. If you are not humble, these experiences will cause you to become puffed up and then you become a candidate for destruction. Pride neutralises the power of prayer. There was an occasion in my church when some of the intercessors went about saying that, without them, the church would be nowhere. This is one of the common deceptions of the devil. When you get to this stage, you forget that somebody brought you up, when you knew nothing at all about Christianity and taught you how to be an intercessor. I find it sad when good believers put on this ugly cloak of pride and think they are indispensable.

- The intercessor must remember that he is a fellow worker with God (1 Cor 3:9). Jesus is our High Priest. He is our Intercessor (Heb 7:25). Our intercession derives from him interceding for us.

- Every intercessor must line up with the vision of the leadership and follow. God cannot operate in an atmosphere of confusion. You may not be happy with everything but it is not your duty to criticise. You have been called by God to pray, so pray!

You have to be mindful about not using your prayer as a weapon to criticise. For instance when you start to say things like, "Last time the pastor did so and so, so let us pray for the pastor so that God will reveal to him that he was wrong." Do not use the intercessory platform as a place to criticise people. That renders your intercession powerless.

• The intercessor must seek only the glory of God.

Openness to correction
• The next qualification of the intercessor is to be open to correction. He must have a teachable spirit. You don't know everything, so when you are wrong, be quick to accept your fault, apologise for your mistake and go ahead with your work. Realise that God is still working on you to bring you to perfection.

Bishop T D Jakes explained it this way: when a stonemason is building a wall, he chips each stone until it fits into its part in the wall. It does not make sense to break down the whole wall and start all over again because of one stone that doesn't fit. So there will be times when, as an intercessor, you will have to be chipped and it will not be comfortable. But hang in there, sooner or later you will become smooth enough, blend in wonderfully, and be a useful tool in the hands of the Lord.

Fellowship in the Word

- Another important qualification is that the intercessor must allow the Word of God to be his master. The Word of God is the basic inexhaustible resource material for the believer to commune with God. Intercession is a two-way conversation. God speaks to us in several ways. The basic way is through his Word. The only way the intercessor can avoid the deception of the devil is to keep to the Word of God and allow his path to be ordered by it (Psalm 119:105; Psalm 119:133; John 14:23). In order for the 'watchman' to stand his ground and perform his duty diligently day and night, he must remain within the borders of the Word of God at all times.

- As an intercessor, you must always be conscious of the grace of God. You may have every capability but without this special ingredient, you will not have any justification to do the task you have given yourself. Desire to be drawn personally to the Lord at all times. Have a personal, ongoing relationship with the Lord and don't just come to his presence when you need to intercede.

Unity, love and hard work

Two important Bible passages are:

PSALM 133:1

How good and pleasant it is when brothers live in unity.

EPHESIANS 4:3

Make every effort to keep the unity of the Spirit through the bond of peace.

God loves unity and it is one of his conditions for him to reveal himself to the local assembly. Unity generates great power (Genesis 11). When there is a lack of understanding among a group of intercessors, it allows the devil to operate among them. They must align themselves with the vision of the leadership of the church. You cannot come into the group with your own agenda. If you believe you have been called to be an intercessor, then place yourself under authority and fall in line with the vision of the house.

According to 1 Corinthians Chapter 13, if you call yourself an intercessor and do not have love, you are "as sounding brass or a tinkling cymbal". This is to say that intercession without love is a nuisance. Which means that if you don't have love you should not attempt to intercede for anyone because you will be wasting your time.

Intercession is hard work. It needs sacrifice. An intercessor must not be lazy. We must wake up early. God desires the first and the best part of everything we have. This includes the day. You can pray at any time, but God is still interested in being the first person you speak to. The 'first fruit' please!

CHAPTER TEN

This is My Story

My father was a nominal Methodist, who went to church on special occasions but was deeply involved in the occult. He depended on the power of witchcraft to protect himself and his household. He was a chain-smoker and enjoyed his booze.

At dawn on my seventh birthday, I was initiated into an occultic ritual. It was a harrowing experience. The throat of a chicken 'without blemish' (with white feathers) was slit and its blood was sprinkled on my instep and I think the lower lobe of my ears.

My father receives Jesus

In 1953, when I was nine years old, my father gave his life to Christ. The change was very dramatic. He immediately stopped his involvement with the occult. He ceased drinking and smoking and he stopped swearing. Even at nine years old, I was aware of the great change.

Our family's life took a new turn. We became deeply involved in church, attending every service. I enjoyed the Sunday school as well and because my name is Samuel, I became very intrigued with the story of Samuel in the Bible. At the age of 14, I was baptised in a river in Accra, Ghana.

As I stayed in church, I noticed that occasionally some people, not many in number though, would pray in tongues and an even smaller number of 'specials' spoke in tongues with interpretation. I presumed it was for some special adults only, so I did not desire the baptism of the Holy Spirit. It did not seem necessary at all.

My first encounter with the Holy Ghost

In 1967, as the President of the Officers Christian Union at the Ghana Military Academy, I led a group of officer cadets from the Academy to an evangelistic meeting at the Baden Powell Memorial Hall in Accra.

At the altar call, I found myself weeping uncontrollably. 'This must not happen to a soldier in public!' I was thinking to myself. As I went forward to the altar, I beckoned to my friends to come up with me but none of them followed me. This was my personal encounter with Jesus. Something happened to me on that day. I did not pray in tongues because, even then, nobody told me that I had that ability when Jesus came into my life. So my mind did not allow me to release that which was inside me.

The bloody coup

When I look back, I now know that encounter in 1967, when I wept uncontrollably in public, was the moment I was baptised in the Holy Spirit. But, although I was baptised in the Holy Spirit in 1967, I did not pray in tongues until 1979, twelve years later. I was serving with the United Nations Emergency Force in the Sinai when another military *coup d'etat* hit my country, Ghana.

It was a very bloody and nasty situation in Ghana. Law and order broke down and senior officers were rounded up and thrown into military prisons, where they were at the mercy of the junior ranks. In fact, several officers were executed.

Speaking in tongues

I was a major commanding a company of about a hundred men in the Sinai Desert. In view of the situation back home and my extreme concern for my family back in Ghana, I organised all-night prayer meetings for interested soldiers within the operational area of my company.

On a particular occasion, as I was driving the soldiers back to their respective locations after the prayer meeting, it dawned on me that I was muttering certain 'strange' words. I still remember the words today. Gradually the words increased in momentum and became louder, so that I could hear myself more clearly. In my mind, I was asking what this could mean. Then these words: "My peace to you, Sophia (my wife) and the boys are fine," replaced the tongues. As I continued to say these words, some inexplicable peace came over me.

Prior to this, all Ghanaian officers of the rank of major and above involved in the Sinai operation were denied mail from Ghana. A miracle happened to me on this very day. One Sergeant Acquah wrote me a letter and, because he was not sure of my address, inserted my letter in another soldier's mail – which was handed to me that same day. That letter contained news about my family. It confirmed what the Holy Spirit had already told me.

I later realised that if God had told me in plain English, I might not have believed it. But when I received the message in tongues with interpretation it put my heart and mind at rest, so I could concentrate on my job.

CHAPTER ELEVEN

Baptism in the Holy Spirit

Praying in tongues is praying with the use of expressions, sounds or languages which are freely given by God and not understood by the one praying. It is one of the gifts God freely blesses us with in Christ Jesus.

EPHESIANS 1:3

Praise be to the God and Father of our Lord Jesus Christ, who has blessed us in the heavenly realms with every spiritual blessing, in Christ.

No man can learn it with his mind. Those believers who believe this blessing and receive it in faith do speak in tongues (Mark 16:17).

You may think that you are a mediocre Christian because you do not speak in tongues. This is not true. We are all children of God. However, God desires that you will also operate in this gift. He freely gave this gift of the Holy Spirit to you from the moment you lifted your hands up and invited Jesus into your life.

When we ask for the baptism of the Holy Spirit, we are saying to God that he should fill all our soul (mind, will and emotion) with his Spirit. That is why, when the Holy Spirit comes, he spreads all over your being and an inexplicable joy wells up inside you.

On several occasions, Jesus talked to the disciples about the promise of the Father to send down the Holy Spirit. The Holy Spirit is equally God and has always been with the Father and the Son. As his work was coming to an end, it was necessary that Jesus prepared his followers for the era of the Holy Spirit.

JOHN 16:7

...It is to your advantage that I go away; for if I do not go away, the Helper will not come to you...

The blessings of the Holy Spirit

1 CORINTHIANS 2:12

Now we have received... the Spirit who is from God, that we might know the things that have been freely given to us of God.

One of the cardinal blessings of the coming of the Holy Spirit is to give us the ability to know the things of the Triune God. He opens our spiritual eyes to understand what God's Word says. He unveils and unravels God's mysteries to us. Therefore, in sending us the Holy Spirit,

God has given us a divine Teacher. He will make us understand the truth.

Jesus emphasised this role of the Holy Spirit when he spoke to his disciples:

JOHN 14:26

But the Helper, the Holy Spirit... will teach you all things...

JOHN 16:13

...The Spirit of truth... will guide you into all truth... he will tell you things to come.

The Holy Spirit comes to also give us power:

ACTS 1:8

But you shall receive power when the Holy Spirit has come upon you; and you shall be witnesses to me in Jerusalem, and in all Judea, and Samaria, and to the end of the earth.

Why do we need power? We need power to be efficient witnesses for the Lord. When we say that Jesus is Lord, what is our proof? There are several gurus who claim to have the secret to life and death. Therefore, we need something more to prove to the world that truly, Jesus is the way, the truth and the life. And that is why the Holy Spirit came.

When Peter and the rest of the disciples walked

with Jesus, they were powerless to profess their knowledge and belief in him. When he was confronted three times as being one of the disciples of Jesus, Peter on each occasion vehemently denied being so, to the extent of even cursing and swearing. His fellow disciples did not even show up, they fled.

Even after Jesus was resurrected, all the disciples remained in hiding because they were scared of the Jews. But a few days after, when the Holy Spirit baptised them, they went boldly into town and Peter stood before the multitudes and told them about the Lordship of Jesus Christ, his resurrection and ascension. The Bible records that 3,000 people were saved there and then (Acts 2:1-22).

Through the baptism in the Holy Spirit we receive power to be true witnesses for the Lord. We receive boldness and authority to preach and the freedom to talk about and demonstrate the love of God through the good news of Jesus.

The blessings of speaking in tongues

A significant sign of the baptism in the Holy Spirit is the ability to speak in other tongues as the Spirit gives us the utterance. The Holy Spirit gives the believer utterance so that he can speak mysteries to God in prayer. This is the same experience the disciples had when they were baptised in Acts 2.

All of them were filled with the Holy Spirit and began to speak in other tongues as the Spirit enabled them.

1 CORINTHIANS 14:2

For he who speaks in a tongue does not speak to men but to God, for no one understands him; however, in the spirit he speaks mysteries.

A lady in my church heard people praying in tongues and she decided to 'learn' it. She thought that I, as the senior pastor, must have the most powerful tongue so she decided to learn the tongues I spoke. At the next service she came with a red pen and a book to write down every word of tongues I spoke. So if I said, "Sha la ka ba," she wrote, 'Sha la ka ba'. In the end she had several pages full so she went home to study. As much as she tried she could not learn it, so in her frustration she decided to leave the church. By God's grace she came with her husband to church one Easter Sunday and I felt led to pray for them. The husband received the baptism immediately. Then, soon after, she also started speaking in tongues whilst rocking a baby during the meeting.

Immediately the service ended, she rushed her husband into their car and dashed home. As soon as she got home, she went on her knees to pray, because she was afraid that she would lose the tongues. Some time later, after she had come to understand the purpose of the baptism of the Holy Spirit and how it operates, she showed me the book with the red writing. You can imagine the great excitement and laughter it caused in church on that day.

Why will God give us a prayer language? The first and most obvious reason is that our natural human language is not able to communicate properly in the spiritual realm. In addition to this failing, our minds control our ability to speak and what we say. When praying in the spirit, there is the need to bypass the mind because spiritual matters are beyond the comprehension of the natural mind. At such times, the mind behaves like a sieve, allowing only things that are familiar to it to come through. However, God wants us to be able to communicate with him beyond this natural plane because in our natural state we are very limited. That is why, when we speak in tongues, we speak another language that is unknown to ourselves but known to God.

When we pray in tongues we also build ourselves up spiritually. In the natural world we are encouraged to walk and exercise our body. Praying in tongues is one sure way of exercising our spirit, thereby building supernatural energy reserves into your relationship and walk with God.

JUDE 20

But you, dear friends, build yourselves up in your most holy faith and pray in the Holy Spirit.

1 CORINTHIANS 14:4

For when I pray in a tongue, my spirit prays, but my mind is unfruitful.

Many times, also, we are limited in our praise and worship. Praying in tongues helps us magnify God.

ACTS 2:11

We hear them declaring the wonders of God in our own tongues.

The miracle on death row

Rev R W Shambach, a renowned evangelist and international speaker, shared this testimony. He was in New York holding a tent crusade when, in the middle of his preaching, a lady raised her hand and started walking forward. He asked her, "What is it Mama?" Then the woman said, "It is half past nine now, at 10 o'clock my son will die in the electric chair, but he is innocent." Rev Shambach replied, "I am sorry Mama, I have visited people on death row, but never anybody with 30 minutes to zero hour. There is nothing I can do."

Then he called on everybody to rise up and asked them to pray in the Spirit. In such a situation if you were praying with your understanding what will you be praying for? Perhaps you will pray that God should console the mother. But when you pray in tongues you leave the wording of the prayer to the Spirit. So the veteran man of God opted for the congregation to pray in other tongues.

Rev Shambach said they prayed and prayed until the place became charged. He wanted to know what he was praying about, so he asked the Holy Spirit for the understanding of the tongues he was speaking. Then he said these words "Holy Spirit find the real offender". Then he looked at the woman and said, "Mama, your son will not die in the electric chair," and dismissed her. He later became aware of what he had just said. But he wished he had not – because he would be coming back into the tent the following evening.

He went back to the hotel and, in the morning, while he was having breakfast, he picked up the New York Times. There in bold print on page three: "Man Saved From The Electric Chair". He said he got right up from where he was and started to dance, oblivious to the fact that people were watching him.

According to the story, the District Attorney (DA) had a phone call from someone who said, "You are going to burn the wrong man". He asked, "How do you know?" Then the caller replied, "I killed the man". He then went on to describe what had happened and gave certain details about the dead body which had not been made public and only the person who had committed the crime would know. The DA asked him, "Where are you?" The man gave him the address and added, "Come and get me." The DA drove quickly and got him.

Later, during interrogation, the man was asked why he gave himself up. This was his reply: "I didn't want to give myself up, but something got hold of me and I couldn't just sit down. So here I am."

The man who was almost executed became born again. What a miracle! Indeed, this man learnt what it is to be truly saved. God literally snatched him from the gates of death. Do you think he will ever quit church?

We need help for our prayer life. For some of us, we have difficulty even in constructing a sentence. So move into praying in the Spirit, so that you can overcome your handicap. Paul said, "I pray with my spirit and I pray with my understanding also..." So you must also pray with your mind and with your spirit. Praying with your spirit involves speaking in tongues. One of the things we have to remember is that praying in tongues does not make a person better than the person who doesn't. Praying in tongues is a gift. We do not earn it!

It is a blessing to have a personal prayer language, which breaks the mind barrier. I was very annoyed when, after twelve years, I found out that I had been blessed with this gift and I had not exercised it. I have determined therefore to teach believers everywhere I go about this free gift and to lead them into possessing it.

I have had several opportunities to do this, but the greatest was when I served on the executive board of Dr Morris Cerullo's 'Mission To London' for four years as the Prayer Chairman. The programme brought together over 450 churches across London. By God's grace we were able to lead several Christians to receive the baptism of the Holy Spirit. My dear brother or sister, ask for and receive the infilling of the Holy Spirit by faith. Thank God for the gift of tongues which the Holy Spirit who dwells within you gives. Begin to exalt and praise God using your own language (and mind) and the spiritual language. Simply believe.

CHAPTER TWELVE

God Wants to Use You!

1 CORINTHIANS 3:16

Do you not know that you are the temple of God and that the Spirit of God dwells in you?

Until Jesus arrived on the scene, God never inhabited human beings. Jesus was the first human being on earth that God could inhabit because he was without sin. Since the fall of our first parents – Adam and Eve – to Satan's deception, man has lived in sin and therefore could not contain the presence of God within him. However, since Jesus came to bear all our sins and die on the cross in our place, our relationship with God has taken a new turn.

All the great Old Testament characters did not have the privilege of being inhabited by God. By God's grace, we have been granted this awesome honour of having the Lord reside within us. So now, when you accept the Lord Jesus as your Lord and personal Saviour, the Lord comes to live inside you. Therefore as a believer your status is now changed. You have been placed in a state where you are justified. Now you have access to God's throne room, so that when you stand to pray, you have direct access to him.

The blood of Jesus pleads for you. Sin has been taken care of. The dominion of sin is broken forever. Therefore, when you declare the oracles of God it shall come to pass. The devil is aware of your position and he will therefore attempt to make you feel inadequate so that you will not put your position to use. Take your stance and put your dynamic power to use. God is calling you to become a prayer warrior – to intercede for your land and its people.

God does not condemn you

As a Christian, you may feel condemned by certain weaknesses in your life. But the Lord was already aware of this before he made you his own. This is why he does not condemn you, but rather calls you to repent of your sin and to get back where you were before you took a wrong turn. His love for you has not changed. It is the devil who condemns. It is the devil's plan to make you feel hopeless. It serves his purpose when he makes you think you cannot make it. This is part of his agenda to make you ineffective. Never be deceived. Do not yield to his agenda of deception.

You see, our state in God is not about who we are or our strength or even our power, but it is by the grace of God. Don't join the condemnation party! Besides the Labour, Conservative or any of the other political parties, there is also the Condemnation Party. Those who belong to it say, "I am not good enough for God to love me. I shall come to him when I am holy enough." This is a clear lie of the devil. Whenever the devil condemns you, his intention is to rob you of the opportunity to be used by God and also to disrupt God's plan for you.

Here is the Lord's answer:

MARK 2:17

I did not come to call the righteous, but sinners, to repentance.

Always remember that you are God's envoy on earth and he intends to affect the earth through you.

2 CORINTHIANS 5:20

We are therefore Christ's ambassadors, as if God was making his appeal through us.

Seeking the peace of our land

JEREMIAH 29:7

And seek the peace of the city where I have caused you to be... and pray to the Lord for it; for in its peace you will have peace.

One Sunday, God gave me a word that made me very frightened. He said, "Europe has turned its back on me and is trusting in technology. Just as the prayers of the afflicted come to me, so have the sins of Europe come to me. If Europe will not turn from this way, I am going to bring about air pollution, water pollution and the spread of skin diseases."

I immediately knew that the Lord had chosen me to intercede on behalf of my land. I knew also that, if Christians did not pray, the devastation prophesied would affect all of us. In giving me this word, God was actually showing concern for fellow Christians in the land so that we would not come to any harm in the future, as we repent and ask for forgiveness on behalf of the land and people of Europe.

Now step out and pray!

God has equipped you with the ability to stand as a warrior for your land, your home and yourself. Always remember that the whole host of heaven is behind you and cheering you on. I pray for you that you will experience the awesome power of prayer as you embark on your journey into greater heights in prayer.

Amen.

PRAISE FOR
THE AWESOME POWER OF PRAYER

Many people teach or write about prayer. Only few actually pray. Pastor Sam Larbie is one of the few who have taken prayer as a lifestyle. He, therefore, writes this book on prayer with deep-seated revelations and experiences, which make this book unique. I recommend it to anyone who wants prayer as a lifestyle.

Dr Spencer Duncan
Senior Lecturer, Haggai Institute
President, Leadership Development Institute

What a unique book on prayer! Highly inspirational and good for revival.

Dr Lawrence Tetteh,
World Miracle Outreach, UK

This challenging publication springs from the heart of a man who carries a clear and powerful anointing. I fully endorse every part of this book that amplifies the need for the Church to rise as a potent intercessory army. It should be read by everyone who is serious about living a courageous and effective Christian life.

John Glass, General Superintendent,
Elim Pentecostal Church

Sam Larbie has taught me more about prayer than anybody else... his life is lived in an attitude of prayer. He has no doubts that, when he prays, God answers. Reading this book has made me want to pray more... Thank you Sam, you have shown me that prayer is the key to life.

Julia Fisher,
Premier Radio